Snapshots of GRACE

Divine Appointments with God

Patty Curl

Tate Publishing & *Enterprises*

Snapshots of Grace

Some names and locations were changed for privacy.

The opinions expressed by the author are not necessarily those of Tate Publishing, LLC.

Published by Tate Publishing & Enterprises, LLC
127 E. Trade Center Terrace | Mustang, Oklahoma 73064 USA
1.888.361.9473 | www.tatepublishing.com

Tate Publishing is committed to excellence in the publishing industry. The company reflects the philosophy established by the founders, based on Psalm 68:11,
"The Lord gave the word and great was the company of those who published it."

Cover design by Kristen Verser
Interior design by Joey Garrett

Published in the United States of America

ISBN: 978-1-61739-096-8
1. Religion / Christian Life / Inspirational
2. Religion / Christian Life / Spiritual Growth
10.10.05

Dedication

To my heavenly Father, for giving my life meaning and purpose. For the gift of His Son, Jesus, and my eternity. For His trust of me with the gifts He has so graciously bestowed. May they be used to His glory.

Acknowledgements

To my husband, Spencer, who opened his heart to let me fly, to the call he let me answer. Thank you, honey; love you always.

To my children, Lori and John, and their spouses who've encouraged and prayed for me, loved me, and given their permission to be a "snapshot of grace." And especially to my son, John, for giving me the title of this book and for letting me share "Our Isaac" and several others from his life. And for both my children's contributions to this work for God, I thank you and love you dearly. Also, my dad and mom, Gene and Frances Lystlund, the best parents anyone could ever have, who've been a huge part of my ministry and pray for me every day, you have my forever love and admiration. My brother and sister-in-law, Jimmy and Jeanette Lystlund. My sister, Debbie Lystlund. All of whom have prayed for my ministry to the Lord through the years and have supported me not only with their prayers but with their financial support. I love you all. I miss you, Debbie, but know you're with the Lord.

To my friends Theresa Williams, Dawson and Hart Smith, Jim and Virginia Ringer, Sabrina Ringer, Jeanne Gibson (for all the photographs she has taken for my CDs and my book), Bob and Laveta Shelton, Candy Thomas, Dona Elliott, Louisa Williams, Carol Green, Rita Pettit, Darrell and Bobbie James, Karen Frazier, Stonecroft Ministries, Forgiven Quartet, Sweet Harmony Trio, Smiley and Nelda Howell, Cathy Minton, Norm Minton, Pastor David Satterfield, Tom and Jane Morris. Additionally, Magdalene Fiallos, Pastor Wesley Goodwin, Alvin and Jackie Sue Mott, Irene Costilow, my Sunday school class at Northeast Baptist Church, and *all* my church families, both at Northeast Baptist Church and my early years at First Assembly of God.

Thank you for supporting and praying for me. Without your obedience, God's call could not have been accomplished.

To my treasured pastor and friend at Northeast Baptist Church, Dr. Larry Nigh, for his prayers and encouragement and his shepherding through teaching God's Word so beautifully.

My friend and minister of music, Guy Cooper, who has blessed me beyond description in the music arena (helping to produce my newest CD, giving unselfishly of his time and talents). For his inspiration to me to continue writing after giving his time to hear some of my "snapshots of grace."

To my Singing Churchwomen sisters who have kept after me to share my stories.

To Jeanette, for her love in typing this book for me and her Lord. For her and my brother Jimmy's permission to share "My Brother's Shoes."

To all whom I have mentioned and those I may have missed, my love, admiration, and gratitude go out to you for your sensitivity to our Lord.

Lord, again my words fall short to express the love I have for You. *You* are my all-in-all.

May *Your* sweet anointing be on every word and every page, to honor You.

Table of Contents

Foreword

S*napshots of Grace* is a divine title for a wonderful book full of spiritual wisdom and insight. Sometimes in life we get overwhelmed by the total picture of an event, situation, or problem and don't know what to do or how to interpret it. But if we take a more focused look at our situation and sense the leadership of God in the moment, we can see the real meaning behind it.

That is what this book is all about. Patty Curl has the unique ability to look at life experiences with spiritual eyes and is able to draw something uniquely special from them that God is trying to teach her. As you read each of these short stories, you too will gain a delightful insight into living as well. If nothing else, it will help you to stop and reflect upon what God is trying to teach you. Life is not always about the *big* picture. More times than not, it is taking the time to see the small, simple, and ordinary things of life where God is at work.

Patty Curl bases her short stories on her personal life experiences and journey with God. She is a gifted speaker, musician, artist, Bible study teacher, and conference leader, and she draws from each of those elements in her attempt to give her readers a wonderful "snapshot of grace."

Each story in her book will grasp your heart and not let go. You'll find yourself not wanting to put the book down until you have read it all the way through.

—Dr. Larry E. Nigh
Senior Pastor
Northeast Baptist Church
Ponca City, OK

Introduction

If you have picked up this book, for whatever reason, you felt drawn to it. Maybe you're asking yourself, "Is God real? If so, can I *really* know Him, and why would He *want* me or *need* me? I don't even know why I'm here in this world. What is my purpose? And what is *Snapshots of Grace: Divine Appointments with God* all about?" Or possibly you've already discovered the reality of God, and you want to hear how others are living their lives with God. I invite you in both endeavors to join me, as I serve only as a signpost.

A snapshot is a picture frozen in time, not the entire happening, but capturing a moment we want to remember. It is a person, a place, or an experience that touches us, one we want to treasure, safely tucked in our hearts. Whether the snapshot is taken with a camera or captured in our mind, we give it a special place in our memories. My dad and mom call those times "making a memory."

So it is with God's grace, too big and too vast to be captured in its entirety. Extraordinary times when God touches mankind and His world with His love and amazing grace. Divine appointments, where God has arranged to meet us right where we are, moments that stay with us forever.

May you find within these pages heartwarming, uplifting stories of my walk with the *One* who loves us most. Follow along with me as He shows me that His promises are true; He will never leave me. Whatever my need, He supplies, because I truly know Him as my Lord and Savior. His love goes farther, wider, and deeper than any other. Yes, they are *divine appointments* where God has met *me,* as He's given me snapshots of His grace.

Even though I grew up in a loving home, attending church three times a week, I discovered I knew *of* God, but I didn't really *know* Him. What I had was a religion, *not* a relationship. I was going through the motions of being what I thought was a Christian.

I share with you some of the disjointed thoughts and questions I struggled with as I was striving to be a good person, all the while not even knowing my own value as a person. I tried to obtain my value and worth from others.

I prayed only when I couldn't accomplish something on my own. Is that all prayer is about?

I was so empty inside. No one knew of my questioning, "Isn't there more than this?"

Maybe you've asked that same question. The answer is "Yes, yes, yes." It's in the *relationship,* and oh, what a difference!

On April 7, 1977, I had arrived at a crisis of belief and needed so much more than just being a pew warmer in church. Nothing was touching me or had any meaning, just words. I didn't know that it was because I didn't know the *author* of that word.

I felt clueless to why I was taking up space in this world or breathing air. All meaning to life, direction, or purpose eluded me; I was so dry and empty inside.

During this time of questioning and searching, I had watched my mother, dad, and sister find a relationship with God, through believing in his Son, Jesus. And seeing the true reality of that relationship in their lives really began to attract my attention.

I remember on that April day yielding my life, such as it was, as I asked Christ to be the Lord of my life, and I had no idea the joy that awaited me. I gave up control to the *One* who had created me.

There was no lightning, thunder, or loud clanging symbols as I made that choice to believe what I had once questioned: "Is God real?"

In that instant, I knew my value as a person. Taking Christ into my heart, the *One* who values me the most, was profound. My journey began.

I found *life,* a rebirth of me.

I felt alive for the first time as I found the Savior. When Christ answered my prayer to take up residence in my heart, He brought His Holy Spirit to dwell there as well, and the Holy Spirit opens your eyes and your ears to truth. And with that came the knowledge of my destination when I leave this world. My reservations for eternity made and confirmed. I met the *Author* of the Book of Life—the Word of God.

I began to marvelously discover that He has a plan and a purpose for me, as He tells me in His word (the Bible) that He will direct my path. Wow! "In all thy ways acknowledge Him, and He will direct thy paths" (Proverbs 3:6 KJV).

Words fail me to adequately describe the experience of finding this love. But as Christ Himself was a storyteller, so too will I strive to tell you, the reader, my story. May you find, as I have found, Jesus *is* who He says He is. He is real and He loves you. Why? Because He chooses to. Whether you accept that love or not, it's still there.

In the pages of this book may you find life. I'm talking *real life.* As I relate my journey, it is my desire that you see only Him as:

The Creator	The healer of your life, body, and soul
The Savior	The Joy Giver
The Comforter	The Teacher
The Shepherd	The Restorer and Rebuilder of lives
The Caretaker of you	The One who died for you

And the Greatest Love of your life

Snow and New Beginnings

Purge me, I shall be clean, wash me, and I shall be whiter than snow.

Psalms 51:7 (NIV)

Snow. What does that word emit from our minds? Think of seeing your first snow as a small child, the excitement it brought.

Snowmen, snowball fights, and even making angels in the snow. Wrapping up in warm clothes and experiencing that first snow of the season.

Drinking hot chocolate by a roaring fire and watching the snow from our windows.

Stepping outside and feeling the coolness of the snowflakes as they rested on our faces. Feeling the quietness, yes, the stillness that snow brings to a noisy world.

As if all sound has stopped—silenced by a blanket of white that can make *all* things seem beautiful.

Thoughts of snow and my view of it changed in a moment of time, like a picture frozen in my memory, when I was given a glimpse of snow as a new beginning—a snapshot of grace.

That Sunday in December started as all Sundays do for me, getting ready to drive into town to attend church. On my usual route into town, I have to pass a junkyard, which isn't a pleasant sight anytime. However, in the spring and summer, when all the trees and shrubs have their foliage on them, it covers most of the ugliness of the scene. But on this wintry day, there were no leaves to hide that ugliness. A discarded junk car sat there, looking old and worn. Maybe once it had a beautiful shine, but now it was rusted and abandoned, past its usefulness to anyone. An old refrigerator sitting next to it, displaying harsh broken edges, covered with filth, leaning to one side, its door ajar, was once the center of someone's kitchen, but it obviously had lost its worth and value. And to complete the grotesqueness of the scene, there in the middle of all that junk stood this old, dead tree. It was so twisted, its totally bare and lifeless limbs extending upward, looking like a scene from a horror movie. As I drove past and glanced that direction, the thought ran through my mind, *What an eyesore; someone needs to clean that up.*

After the church service, while getting my coat I'd hung next to a window, I looked out and saw it had snowed. I stepped outside and breathed deeply, wanting to experience the freshness it had given the air.

On my drive home, my thoughts were far from the new snow, only on planning what to cook for dinner. I drove past the junkyard and glanced in its direction, and oh, what a difference.

The beauty of it was almost overwhelming.

I pulled my car over to the side of the road, wanting to linger there for a while. I thought, *How could such ugliness become so breathtakingly beautiful?* The *only* thing that had changed—it had snowed. I sat there staring, trying to take it all in.

My eyes were drawn to looking at each player in that scene of beauty. The old junky, rusted out car was now covered with a blanket of pure, white, sparkling snow, and it took on the appearance of an object purposefully sculpted with great care. Then I moved my gaze to the old refrigerator and saw that its harshness and filth had been softened and cleansed by the pristine snow, given the same purposeful care. Its value now was its graceful beauty. And there stood that tree, once seemingly so lifeless and dead, having not a thing to offer this world any longer. But the snow had changed all that, for now it had a beautiful white shawl of snow draped around it, and the limbs seemed stretched toward heaven in praise.

I whispered a prayer in my heart, *Lord, how can something as simple as snow make such a difference?* The Lord of creation, speaking to my heart in the quietness and stillness of the moment, said, *It's the same with My children. Their lives are so twisted and full of junk and filth, seemingly dead, having nothing to offer, no value, discarded by the world. But when they find My Son and accept Him as their Savior, He forgives them, and His blood covers them; they become white as snow.*

I call encounters like these *divine appointments* with our Creator, when God interrupts our lives to touch our hearts to see ourselves and others as He sees us.

Just as snow brought beauty, cleanness, and freshness to that junkyard, so too can the Lord change us and make us white as snow, give us newness of life, and yes, new beginnings, as our lives can be purposefully sculpted by God, who created the heavens and the earth, hung the stars, and made all things beautiful.

> When someone becomes a Christian he becomes a brand new person inside. He is not the same anymore. A new life has begun.
>
> 2 Corinthians 5:17 (TLB)

I Almost Missed Her

> For I am convinced that nothing could ever separate us from His love. Death can't, and life can't. The angels won't, and all the powers of hell itself cannot keep God's love away.
>
> Romans 8:38 (TLB)

I've learned that when God wants to teach us something, I find it always has a multipurpose lesson. In this story I share a lesson on forgiveness and keeping your heart right.

One evening someone knocked on our door while I was busily loading the dishwasher. I went to answer the door. There stood a young man I recognized who had worked with my husband some years earlier in another state. He was visiting our town and stopped in to see us. He introduced his girlfriend and a little boy with him to Spencer and me. Much to my chagrin, both adults were carrying open containers of beer. Because of many hurts associated with alcohol abuse, fear and disgust rose up within me, and letting these people into my home was the *last* thing I wanted to do. I was offended that they had the nerve to bring alcohol into my house.

Adding to my disgust, the young woman was scantily dressed: a blouse that was too low, shorts that were too short and so tight they looked painted on. And she had an eye-popping figure, which my husband took definite note of. So the green-eyed monster was having a heyday with me too.

Spencer showed them to the living room. I, on the other hand, headed to the kitchen to continue loading the dishwasher, for visiting with them wasn't what *I* wanted to do.

Are you sensing just a touch of a bad attitude here? As I angrily shoved the dishes into the dishwasher, God began to deal with my heart, reminding me that Jesus wouldn't be treating guests this way. Feeling guilt rush over me, I prayed, *Lord, help me. I know I shouldn't be acting this way, but this reminds me of all the hurts alcohol has caused in the life of my family.*

As I finished the prayer, the little boy walked into the kitchen, opened my refrigerator, began taking food out, and walked back into the living room with a handful of lunchmeat.

Of course, this added to my anger—*you think?* It seemed as if Satan had decided to test my mettle.

Once again, the child returned, opened the fridge (never asking permission), and took *more* food back into the living room. *Good grief, don't they feed this kid?* I thought. I followed him into the living room this time to see what he was doing with the food and wished I hadn't. He was *smearing* it all over my furniture. I retreated to the kitchen. He came back for another visit, so I asked him, "Son, don't you need to ask your dad if you can have that?"

"That isn't my dad."

"Oh. Well, is that your mom?"

He nodded yes and was gone, with grapes this time.

His mother never *once* tried to correct his behavior and allowed him to continue ruining the furniture. Then the child, who had mud all over his little cowboy boots, started climbing on the furniture. *Great. He's getting mud everywhere.* Still, no response from the mom.

Okay, I'm just about done. Stick a fork in me 'cause I'm done. The prayer I had prayed in the kitchen was becoming a distant memory, for terrible thoughts of anger were looming in the forefront of my mind.

I walked back into the living room to give being nice another try, just in time to see the little boy kick over his mother's open can of beer that was sitting on the floor. Obviously, Satan wasn't satisfied that he'd tested me enough. I watched the beer flowing freely out onto my carpet. I stood there speechless while I watched it spread.

I knew at that instant I had a choice. I could show all the anger I was feeling, *or* I could reflect the love of Christ in my life, which up to now I had been hiding pretty well, unfortunately.

The choice was mine. What was more important, my feelings or the people?

After cleaning up the beer from the carpet, I walked out of the room and headed to my music room.

I returned with my music album, one the Lord had provided for me to make some months previously. It was a true blessing because I was able to make it at the Gaither Studio in Indiana. One of my paintings graced the album cover, another blessing from a loving God. Now I needed to show that same love. I handed the album to the young woman, saying, "I want to share with you what Christ has done in my life."

She looked up at me and said, "I would love to hear about it."

What a turn of events. I can honestly tell you that at that precise moment, I felt such love for her, and I knew God had brought her to my home. All of that anger, judgmental attitude, jealousy, and hurt were replaced instantly with eyes that saw her as Jesus was seeing her. I no longer saw her outward appearance. I saw her as a person whom Christ had died for, someone of worth and value.

The men took the little boy to go outside, leaving the two of us alone. I began to share how I found Christ, how I had felt of little value, never quite measured up, and how after I accepted Christ as my Savior, He began to unfold meaning, purpose, and direction to my life. He truly had something for me to do in this world. I told her He was the God of second chances, that He forgives our past and wipes the slate of our life clean—we get to start over.

I must have hit a nerve. She started crying, so I went to her and put my arms around her, trying to comfort her. She started sharing deep, hurtful things from her life, and she told me she was planning on ending her life when they returned home. She revealed that she'd been raped only a few weeks before while her boyfriend was at work. Someone broke into her bedroom in the middle of the night, attacked her, and then was gone. She had no idea who it was. She'd never told anyone, not even her boyfriend, but she said she felt dirty and worthless because she'd not lived a very good life and was ashamed. She thought there was no way out. There was just too much junk in her life and no hope for a future to be anything different. She felt dead inside.

But then she said, "Patty, you've shown me what I've been looking for, a way to become a new person, as you said, to start over with a clean slate. I didn't know that was possible."

I told her how much God loved her, that He gave His Son to die for her while she wasn't living right. Also, I told her, as the scripture says, "For *all* have sinned and come short of the glory of God" (Romans 3:23 TLB, italics mine).

I told her *all* means *all* of us who've ever breathed air. We've been selfish with our lives, walking our own paths instead of the path God has for us. He wants to be our Father.

She left my home knowing of a Savior, a new-found truth of her purpose as God's child, and new beginnings.

Her lesson from the Lord was, "Behold I will make all things new" (Revelation 2:15 KJV).

My lesson: there was a hidden unforgiveness in my heart for hurts associated with alcohol abuse, one the Lord knew lingered in my heart, and for me to be truly free to walk in forgiveness, that needed to be dealt with.

So He brought a young woman to my house to address those hurts that produced that unforgiveness so I could be tested to see it there and to make the choice to forgive, see past it, and see a dying soul right in front of me. She was one who stood on the edge of destruction, and God sent her to me. So I asked God to forgive me for holding hurts in my heart, and He did.

What a humbling experience—*I almost missed her.*

I was so blinded by hurt and anger, but God in His infinite mercy brought the two of us together for a moment in time, to save her and to cleanse my heart. It was truly a new beginning for both of us.

We stayed in touch for a while. She got involved in a church, she and the young man got married, and the little boy now has a sister. I've lost track of her, but I know because of our time together God is with her wherever she is.

Thank you, Lord, for giving us that snapshot of grace and for keeping Your divine appointment.

> What a wonderful God we have, He is the Father of our Lord Jesus Christ, the source of every mercy, and the One who so wonderfully comforts and strengthens us in our hardships and trials. And why does He do this? So that when others are troubled, needing our sympathy and encouragement, we can pass on to them this same help and comfort God has given us.
>
> 2 Corinthians 1:3, 4 (TLB)

The Anniversary Napkins

Let Him have all your worries and cares, for He is always thinking about you and watching everything that concerns you.

1 Peter 5:7 (TLB)

As most would agree, a 50th wedding anniversary is something to celebrate. It is a genuine milestone of life, with memories to be shared, including laughter and tears. It's a time of gathering loved ones to embrace each other and celebrate the part each played in those years.

On June 4, 1991, my dad and mom had reached that day, a day of joy and anticipation of seeing all those they had loved and cared about over the years now coming together in honor of their marriage and lives.

Their children, the three of us, wanted everything to be perfect for the day. We divided the responsibilities of the preparations with great care. As the time drew closer for my husband and me to make the long car trip to my parents' home, I reflected on how thankful I was that I had been a part of the planning for their day. Since I lived a thousand miles away, I spent many hours on the phone with caterers to get it all done, certainly not an easy task but a labor of love for me. To make it simpler, I had the invitations printed in my hometown. Also, the anniversary napkins were ordered, with my parents' favorite colors and pertinent engraving, with plans to transport them when we made the trip.

The invitations were mailed, and the beautiful napkins were ready to be packed in our car for the trip—all 350 of them.

My husband's routine was to pack the trunk of the car the night before leaving; then in the morning we only needed to load our overnight bag and our ice chest, which we'd use along the way for snacks and drinks. After packing the car, we retired for the night.

That night I had a dream, one so vivid the realness of it to me could not be argued. I awoke the next morning with the dream still fresh on my mind, as I'd dreamed it over and over all night long. I don't dream a lot, so when I *do* dream it's usually for a reason.

Cautiously, I began to share the dream with my husband at breakfast because I knew the result of my sharing would include a request for the repacking of the trunk of our car, a task I knew he wouldn't be happy about. So I forged ahead, relating the dream to him.

"Honey," I said, "I had a dream last night that on our trip today we were going to drive in rain and the trunk leaked, ruining the boxes of the anniversary napkins. So could you please unpack the trunk and move them to a safer place?"

He looked at me with disbelief and said, "Blondie," (usually a term of endearment but today not so much), "do you expect me to unload that trunk *because of a dream?*"

I answered, "Uh huh."

"That car is practically new. It's *not* going to leak, so forget it."

As I continued to bat my eyes like a sad little puppy, I again begged him to reconsider.

Finally, he said, "You're not gonna let me alone about this, are you?"

I said, with a smile, "Probably not."

Well, with that thought looming in his mind he trudged outside, with reluctant steps to unload the trunk that he had so carefully and painstakingly arranged the night before. I heard words coming out in the form of mumblings that I probably didn't want interpreted, if you know what I mean.

Napkins found, he asked where I wanted them. I stated, "I want them in the backseat of the car, safe and dry." He looked with raised eyebrows, but complied with my request.

Naturally, we were late leaving due to the unexpected delay caused by my dream, but the day was a nice day of driving, and much to my surprise, there was no rain, nary a drop.

It was getting late in the day, and we'd driven at least halfway to our destination, so we decided to stop for the night. Having made this trip many times over the years, routinely we'd get a motel room. We'd walk inside the room to be sure it was to our liking; then he'd go back out to unload our overnight bag from the trunk, bringing it into the room. So he left to go back out to the car.

Time passed, more time passed, and he still hadn't returned to the room.

I began to get concerned, so I walked to the door, opened it, and saw there by our car *all* of our luggage, out on the sidewalk. *All* the contents of the trunk were now taken out. And there, in all his glory, was my husband, standing there holding the mat from the bottom of the trunk and it was *dripping wet. Dripping,* I emphasize. I looked at him, saying, "Honey, isn't that the mat from the trunk?"

"Don't even start with me. It didn't rain, and the trunk didn't leak."

I smiled, and gently asked, "So what happened?"

"The plug came out of the ice chest and flooded the trunk."

Very lovingly, I said, "Boy, it's a good thing you moved those napkins, isn't it?"

We both started laughing, and I realized we'd been a part of another snapshot of grace—how God tells us that He is concerned with whatever concerns us, and nothing is too small a concern for Him to take notice of, even 50th anniversary napkins.

Yes, I will bless the Lord and not forget the glorious things He does for me.

Psalm 103:2 (TLB)

On the Right Path

> And I am sure that God, who began a good work within you, will keep right on helping you grow in His grace until His task within you is finally finished until that day when Jesus Christ returns.
>
> Philippians 1:6 (TLB)

To follow Christ in all areas of my life is the desire of my heart. All He's done to keep me ever in His care constantly amazes me. He knows how important it is to me that I stay on His path, so I share how I received that assurance.

Working at a full-time job for two years to supplement our family income was a new role for me. I'd been a stay-at-home mom for sixteen years. At my job I was beginning to feel restless, sensing God wanted me to do more with my singing for Him. We'd become dependent on my income, so it was a scary prospect to give that up to pursue a path I'd felt drawn to.

I had sung since age six at many events, churches, and nursing homes throughout the years on a voluntary basis; however, my singing was a small part of my life, never viewed or pursued as a career.

I talked it over with my husband, Spencer, and he said he'd support me in whatever endeavor I felt I needed to do. The Lord seemed to have definite plans for me, plans I'd never dreamed of. As the scripture says, "Now to Him who is able to do exceeding abundantly beyond all that we ask or think" (Ephesians 3:20 KJV).

Giving two weeks' notice to my employer, I gave up my job to wait on the Lord as to what was to be my next move.

As the days passed, some doubt and fear began to assault my resolve. Had I really heard God? Did I do the right thing?

Almost a month passed. Deciding out of fear, no doubt, that God must surely need my help to get things moving, I took another job. Money was getting tight.

I received training for this new position then stepped into the actual workday of performing the job. I had never been a smoker. In fact, I'd had severe allergic reactions to even being around cigarette smoke. Now I found myself surrounded by ten other workers, nine who smoked. Not a good situation to put one's self in. Obviously, trying to help God out put me in a precarious place. Sore throats, laryngitis, and lung infections are the enemy of a vocalist. My leading from the Lord, as I understood it, was for me to *expand* my singing abilities into full-time ministry. So here I was, no one to blame but myself for getting into a bad situation because of my impatience with God's timetable. After only three weeks I quit, knowing this wasn't where I was supposed to be. Again, I stayed home to wait.

At this point in my story, I'd love to be able to tell you that I was now willing to wait as long as it took, but that was not the case. Once again, I decided to help God to get things moving a little faster. I took a job as a salesperson for a cosmetic line. Yep, I did it. I'm sure God must have been thinking, *Here she goes again.* But this was a job I could do from home, making my own hours and still leaving time for God's plan, right? *Wrong!* Are you getting a sense that I wasn't trusting God to come through? *Hello!* He has such a sense of humor, loving me even in my stupidity, and can make His point in the most creative and unexpected ways.

In church one Sunday evening, realizing what a mess I'd created by not trusting and unsure how to fix the mess, my thoughts were interrupted by the youth pastor who was speaking. He began by telling a joke. A man went hiking, and he got too close to the edge of a cliff and fell off. On his way down, he spotted a little limb jutting out from the side of the cliff. In desperation he grabbed on to the tiny limb, the only thing keeping him from falling to his death. As he hung there wondering if the little limb would hold him, he began to call out for help, "Is anyone up there? I need help." He heard a booming voice say, "Yes, son, I hear you." The man said, "God, is that you?" The voice replied, "Yes, son, I'll help you." Then the man said, as he dangled precariously, "What do you want me to do,

God?" God replied, "The first thing I want you to do, son, is trust Me. The second thing I want you to do, let go of the limb." The man yelled, "Uh, is there anybody else up there?" The congregation roared with laughter, as did I. But the punch line of that joke hit its mark straight to my heart. God was telling me, "Patty, let go of the limb, trust Me; I'll catch you." I hadn't been willing to trust Him that He would not let me fall.

Lesson finally learned, I gave up all job pursuits; I waited. With that commitment on my part, peace came, His peace.

A few days later, I decided to share with my pastor at First Assembly, David Satterfield, about my leading from God and the lesson I'd learned the hard way over the past weeks. He listened, smiled, and said, "I'd love to help you get started in a full-time singing ministry, if you'd let me. I'd like to sponsor a concert for you right here at the church, and I'll contact other churches in the state to book you for concerts. How does that sound?"

Flabbergasted, I said, "Are you serious? My gosh, I'm overwhelmed! Thank you! I just came to visit with you; I sure didn't expect this."

"Well, as you were telling me, God began showing me He wanted me to help you get started, so I'm excited to be part of this."

So it began. God had moved in His timing to launch me into a full-time singing ministry. However, new surprises and blessings awaited me.

Concert dates set, things moving forward, I again met with my pastor to solidify the plans.

While discussing the different churches where I'd been booked to sing, he told me that some of the churches didn't have adequate sound equipment. He asked if I had my own. I told him that I didn't, and even if I had it, I wouldn't have any idea how to operate it. The pastor continued, "I know of some sound equipment you can borrow. It belongs to my son. He has a band but isn't using the equipment right now, and I'll teach you how to operate it."

I was beginning to see the path.

A quote from Charles Spurgeon says it all, "God doesn't call the equipped; He equips the called."

For several years, God opened doors across the country for me to sing. Many hearts were touched by Him through the music, and He was meeting our family needs through love offerings from the churches. The borrowed equipment had been a wonderful blessing; however, the pastor's son who owned it had started his band again and needed it. Expecting the time to come when I'd need to return it, I'd been pricing equipment to purchase. I knew exactly the pieces required and was given a quote of $1,300 at a music store in a nearby town.

One morning as I was making my bed, singing songs to make the task go faster, I felt the Holy Spirit nudge my heart, *Go get your sound equipment.* It was a strong nudge, getting my attention, as I certainly hadn't been thinking about doing that at all. Just so you know, I don't immediately jump when I'm nudged like that. I do question, as I did that day. Was this really the Lord speaking to me, and where was the $1,300 going to come from that I'd need to make the purchase?

Now seems a good time to address a pertinent scripture. Jesus said, "My sheep hear My voice, and I know them" (John 10:27 KJV). Your relationship with Christ is like the best of friendships, and like friendships, the more time you spend together, the more you'll know them and recognize their voice.

So it is with Christ. When He speaks to me through His Holy Spirit, the Bible, or through circumstances, I've come to recognize His voice. I've walked with Him since I was thirty-three years old, and He's taught me all along those years to listen, to hear, and to know.

Do I always get it right? No, I'm definitely a work in progress, but my trust has really grown and continues to grow day by day.

Even though I might question, I do wait for the peace to come before I move ahead. I also seek agreement of my spirit with God's spirit. I additionally seek by husband's agreement, as he's my life partner. God has used my husband as a check-and-balance in my life, and for that, I'm thankful. All bases covered, I forged ahead.

Heading out of town to the music store where I'd received the $1,300 quote, while reviewing the list of things I'd need, a music tape was playing in my car. Suddenly, the tape broke. It was one of my accompaniment tapes I used in my concerts, so it was necessary to get it repaired quickly.

Taking a detour to a stereo shop in my town became the first order of business. The sound equipment would have to wait a little longer.

A friend had told me about this store, stating they repaired and spliced broken cassette tapes. Arriving there, I noticed they sold and installed car stereos. An employee took my tape and headed to the back of the store to repair it. A man identifying himself as the store manager struck up a conversation with me while I was waiting. He asked if I'd been helped, and I told him yes and explained why I'd stopped at the store. We talked about the weather and other friendly exchanges, when he asked, "So are you just out enjoying the day?" I told him where I was headed when the tape broke and what I'd intended to buy at the music store. He asked what kind of sound equipment I needed. I showed him the list of pieces, along with the price quote. He said, "You know, I can order the exact equipment, and I'm pretty sure I can beat that price."

"You can order music equipment to perform with?"

"Yes, I sure can. In fact, I order my car stereos from the same distributor. Why don't you go have lunch and come back in an hour? We'll have your tape repaired, and I'll have a quote for you that'll beat the other one, and it'll save you an out-of-town trip." I left in amazement, wondering if God had interrupted my plan to put me on the right path.

When I returned to the stereo shop, the manager met me, saying, "I can get you the same equipment, all the pieces on your list, for $875. That's $425 less than the $1,300. Does that sound reasonable?"

My response was, "Wow."

The path grew clearer.

Overcome with gratitude to the *One* who had orchestrated this, I had the store manager place the order. It would arrive in two weeks.

Driving home, my mind was reeling at the wonder of a great God who chose to be so personally involved in my life. Growing up, I'd had so many misconceptions about God. I thought He'd be harsh and judgmental, just waiting to punish when we messed up. I never knew you could really know Him while alive on earth and thought that you'd only meet Him when you died. Most certainly, you couldn't know Him in a personal way. All of that was so wrong. I've found Him to be a loving God, a true Father to His creation, and I realize the entire Bible is about God trying to bring man back to Himself.

More thoughts were running through my mind. We humans are like grains of sand. There are millions and millions of us, yet the God who created the universe and all it contains wants to meet *my* need. Think on that; try to wrap your mind around it.

Reality hit. I was nearing my house as a thought occurred to me, *I don't have $875, and I don't know if I'll have it in two weeks.* I argued with myself back and forth. *Believe, trust God, for He just did a wonderful thing; trust. But where's the money going to come from?* I decided to head back into town and go to our bank to ask for a loan. *Say what?*

Okay, let's look at what God's doing here. He's leading, guiding, giving wisdom, courage, and strength to do something I'd never done before. Step-by-step He was laying out the path before me.

I was greeted by the receptionist at the bank asking me how she could help me. I asked, "Could I talk to someone about a loan, please?"

She replied, "All of our loan officers are busy, but our vice president would be happy to talk to you." Here I was, scared to death to talk to a loan officer, and now I was being offered the vice president. Oh, Lord!

I told the receptionist, "Okay, I guess that'll be all right." She led me to his office, and he extended his hand and called me by name. I had given no one my name, so how did he know me?

The plot thickens.

The bank vice president asked what I needed today. Swallowing hard, I began. "I need a loan to buy some sound equipment."

"What's the amount you need?"

"$875."

He smiled. "I think that's doable. How much would you like your monthly payments to be?"

I've run out of adjectives to express my awe that day standing in the vice president's office.

I looked at him and said, "You're going to loan me the money? Well, I need to tell you that I don't have a job."

He grinned and said, "Patty, I attended one of your concerts, and I'm behind you 100 percent in what you're doing for the Lord. We will need your husband's signature on the note with yours, but I'm happy to loan you what you need so more people can hear you sing and share your testimony. I can tell you it touched my life." Whoa, was that great or what? I told him that I'd wondered how he knew my name then thanked him for his encouragement and said I was so glad the music had blessed him.

We agreed on a monthly payment of $80, which at that moment I didn't know where it would come from either, but I was now recognizing (better late than never) that this was God's doing and He'd complete what He'd started.

Arriving home, riding on cloud nine (maybe even ten), I'll admit I was a little fearful of telling my husband I had applied for a loan without first talking to him about it. I wasn't sure if he'd be angry when I told him, and then I had to ask him to cosign the note.

Spencer came home. I was waiting in the kitchen. He gave me a hello kiss with a look of excitement on his face. He said, "I've got something to tell you, Blondie."

"You do? Well, I've got something to tell you too."

He said, "Okay, you go ahead."

Since I wasn't in any hurry to share, I asked him to go first. He began, "Well, I got a good raise today, a cost-of-living raise. It was more than I'd expected, so I'm giving you $25 more a month than the money I usually give you, and you can use it for anything you like."

All right, things were looking better. Now I had $25; I only needed $55.

So it was my turn to share. I started by hugging Spencer, hopefully preparing his heart. You female readers understand how that show of affection can't hurt, right? "Honey," I began, "thank you for the extra money. I'm so happy about your raise, and I'm proud of you too. You certainly deserve it."

"Okay, so what do you need to tell me?"

I pulled up my big-girl pants and began, "Remember I'd talked to you about the sound equipment?" He nodded, I continued, "Well, I found a store today that can get the same stuff for only $875 instead of the $1,300. Isn't that great?" He nodded, I went on. "So I told the guy at the store to order it, and it'll be here in two weeks, and I was thinking of a way I could pay for it." He nodded. "So I went to our bank and asked for a loan."

At this point I stepped back a little. Without a pause to breathe, I said, "My payments will be $80 a month. I've got a card for you to sign, and I got to talk to the vice president of the bank about the loan. Isn't that something?"

He nodded then started to speak. "Blondie, I know it took a lot of guts for you to do that, and I'm proud of you, *but* I don't want you to make a habit of getting loans without talking to me first. Understand?" I nodded. Spencer continued, "I'll sign the note and return it to the bank tomorrow."

"Okay. So I'm going to use the $25 toward the $80."

"Where are you going to get the other $55?"

"I don't have a clue, but I'm trusting God to provide, because He's obviously clearing the path for all these things to have happened."

While Spencer was adding his signature to the card, standing by our kitchen window, he noticed someone driving up to the house and said, "Hey, one of your friends just drove up." I met her at the back door, we hugged, and I invited her into the living room, asking what she was doing in Ponca City that day.

"Patty, you're going to think this is strange, but in my prayer time this morning, the Lord laid it on my heart that I was to give you $50 a month for something you needed. So here's my first check, and I have to ask you something. Do you know what it's for?"

I burst out laughing, and so did Spencer. "I sure do know what it's for, but I can't take that." I pointed to her check.

"Oh, yes you can. If you don't take it, you're cheating me out of a blessing." That pretty much settled the matter since I surely didn't want to keep her from being blessed. I shared the whole day's events with her. She was thrilled God had made her a part of His plans. I was thankful to her for hearing and being obedient.

A clearer view of the path.

So I was thinking, *Okay, Lord, you've gloriously supplied. I have $75 of the $80 needed. I only need $5, and I can afford to pay that myself.*

But that was not in His wonderful plan. There's a scripture in the Old Testament that says, "Not by might, nor by power, but by My spirit says the Lord" (Zechariah 4:6 KJV).

Every month I received, in my mailbox, a plain white envelope with my name typed on the front—no address, no return address, just my name. The envelope was sealed, and as I opened it, it held a folded piece of paper with a typed scripture verse and a crisp, new $5 bill. I received one every month until the loan was paid in full. (Are you thinking *wow* yet? Me too. I lived it, and it's still a wow.) God is faithful. He *does* complete what He started.

I questioned many people to see if they had placed the envelope in my mailbox every month. No one admitted to doing it, but even so, I cannot say that I don't know where it came from, because *I do* know.

It came from my heavenly Father who wanted me to know that I was on His path, *the right path.*

He called,

I answered,

He equipped—all glory is His.

> Then everyone will be praising the name of the Lord Jesus Christ because of the results they see in you, and your greatest glory will be that you belong to Him. The tender mercy of our God and of the Lord Jesus Christ has made all this possible for you.
>
> 2 Thessalonians 1:12 (TLB)

> God has given each of you some special abilities, be sure to use them to help each other, passing on to others, God's many kinds of blessings.
>
> 1 Peter 4:10 (TLB)

A personal, loving relationship is something we all desire and need. Of all the religions in the world, only God has pursued that *personal* relationship with man. He wants to be involved in your day-to-day life, to not only love you but provide for you and give meaning to your existence that will bring joy into your life beyond your wildest dreams. So count your blessings and take nothing for granted; He chooses to make you a part of something much bigger than yourself.

A wonderful example of that for me was when God expanded my path. He graciously gifted me with a speaking ministry along with my singing ministry and later gave me the ability to become an artist. He has set my course; my path is to live, sing, and speak for Him, wherever He opens doors. He has made me a part of something bigger than myself, something that has eternal value. And that brings me joy beyond measure.

My Brother's Shoes

Every good and perfect gift is from above, coming down from the Father of the heavenly lights, who does not change, like shifting shadows.

James 1:17 (NIV)

There are times in our lives when we are provided the opportunity to give back or say the thank yous that were never really said. Such is the case in this story I share with you about my brother's shoes.

My brother, Jimmy, and I have always had a special bond. He's eighteen months older than I, but when we were younger, people would ask if we were twins. As happens with many families, in our adult years, our lives took us down different roads and to different areas of the country. Many miles separated us, and everyday living and raising our families replaced the closeness we'd experienced as children. But in 1994, our roads of life would once again converge in a very special and wondrous way.

In the 1990s, many people experienced being downsized from large companies and corporations. My brother was one of those casualties. I'd heard about how devastated Jimmy was through a conversation with our parents. Like most people who found themselves out of a job as a result of the downsizing process, Jimmy was in his fifties. He'd always been a wonderful provider, marvelous at his job, more than competent in everything he did. He was a giving person in so many ways to his family, his friends, his church, and to people he hardly knew, reaching out to help whenever he saw a need. Although highly educated, having graduated from high school and college at the top of his class and successfully climbed the corporate ladder, he found that he was in a strange, scary, and very humbling place. He began to search in earnest for other employment in his field, coming face-to-face with others seeking the same jobs he sought.

Weeks, then many months, passed. He tried reinventing himself and his skills, being somewhat successful, but his former salary and job prestige remained elusive. His family was very supportive. Jeanette, his wife, who also worked, carried most of the financial burden at this trying time in their lives. Decisions had to be made so as not to lose their home. They were also trying to provide a way to keep both their children in college. I'd always heard that you really know what a person is made of when they are squeezed, just wait to see what comes out.

Putting pride aside, they decided to move in with Jeanette's mother. As can be imagined, the pressures on my brother as a husband, a provider, and a father began to take their toll. He was being squeezed from all sides, as was Jeanette. Yet their faith in God remained strong and was of great comfort to them, even though it seemed their world as they had known it was crumbling around them.

As time passed, I was more and more drawn to be a part of Jimmy's life once again, to be there for him as he'd always been there for me as my big brother, my protector, my defender, my supporter. But I'd never known him to be the one in need. My heart broke for him. I began to call more often to encourage, to listen, and to pray. A new role for us both, our roads were converging, but for what reason, I didn't know. In our conversations, I could hear despair creeping in. I wanted desperately to help him, but how?

The holidays were approaching, and we'd discussed the possibility of us all going home for Christmas, home being Georgia, where our parents and sister lived and where we'd grown up. All those warm thoughts that the holidays usually bring were being mingled with the uncertainty of the days ahead. As I spoke with Jimmy about meeting for Christmas, he began to share things with me that he had chosen not to tell our parents, to not worry them with the true circumstances he was facing. As he poured out his heart, he told me of his "interview shoes," which were now beginning to show holes from his many months of pounding the pavement in his efforts to find the same financial security he'd provided for his family in the previous years. He'd work at other jobs, some in the day, some at night, also on weekends, and job hunt in between.

I was experiencing so many emotions as I listened to him. I longed to put my arms around my brother to comfort him, to help him, but what could *I* do? My prayer became, "Lord, help me to help him. Show me how."

Even as I was saying this prayer, words kept running through my head about God making a way, somehow, someway. Then my thoughts turned to what Jimmy had *just* told me—he needed shoes. I could do that for him. *All right,* I thought, *that will be my surprise Christmas present to him.* But he still had to agree to meet in Georgia for Christmas. Would he? Our conversation continued. I said, "Jimmy, what kind of shoes *are* your interview shoes?"

"Well, they're wingtips. Why are you asking?"

"Oh, I was just curious." Then I turned to encouraging him about going home for Christmas and how wonderful it would be for all of us to be together. I *knew* finances were affecting his decision, so I interjected, "You know, Christmas is all about celebrating Christ's birth, being together, and loving one another, not about presents anyway, so how about it?" He said he would think about it and let me know.

Now, I had a mission, a way to help, a way to give back.

A few days later, I was preparing to go out of state on a speaking engagement. The phone rang, and my mom said she'd just talked to Jimmy, and he and the family *were* coming for Christmas. My heart leapt into my throat, it was coming together. I could see him, hug him, and give him his shoes, the meaning of which would only be known to him, me, and God; who was arranging all of this.

Now I knew I had to begin to search with fervor for wingtip shoes, whatever those were, for I didn't have the first idea. I began getting even more excited about Christmas. I didn't know exactly how God would do it, but I knew He was going to do something wonderful. God was preparing a snapshot of grace.

The search was on. I soon discovered wingtips are a somewhat expensive shoe, well beyond my budget, but I was determined to continue looking. In every town I spoke, I went to shoe stores, only to be disappointed. Then I was taken to a mall while out of state in Kansas City. I tried their shoe stores to no avail. Finding just the right shoes for just the right price was becoming a tall order. As I was exiting the mall, I saw a tiny shoe store stuck in a corner, one I had overlooked. I was tired and almost ready to give up, but I remembered how much it would mean if I found them. So in I went. As I searched the store, I caught a glimpse of a pair of wingtips sitting by themselves on a lower shelf. They were just the right color, a beautiful burgundy. I thought, *Could these be the right size?*

A few days prior to leaving for my trip, just to be safe, I had called my parents to inquire if Jimmy's shoe size was the same as it used to be, nine and a half B, the same as Dad's. My dad said, "Yes, as far as I know, it is. Why do you want to know that?"

I said, "I just want to give Jimmy a gag gift for Christmas," remembering my promise to Jimmy not to tell our parents about his shoes being so worn.

I started looking for the salesman in the shoe store after having checked the size on the shoes and seeing they weren't the right size. I wanted to see if they had them in the same color, size nine and a half B, and for sure at a price *I* could afford. The salesman approached, asking if I needed help. I responded, "Would you have this same shoe in a size nine and a half B?"

"Let me go look."

As he was walking away, I said, "By the way, how much are they?"

"Well, we're having a big clearance on this style shoe. They've been marked down three times, so today they are $49.95."

To say I was excited would be an understatement, as $175 and up was the regular price for wingtips. So I held my breath as he went to look for the nine and a half B shoes.

He returned with a box in his hands and said, "Okay, you're in luck today. I've got one pair left in that size. Do you want them?"

Did I want them? I knew it wasn't luck at work here. I walked to the counter to pay for the shoes as the salesman began to close the box. I said, "I sure hate to ask you to do this, but I'm from out of state. I live in Oklahoma, and I'm taking these to Georgia as a Christmas present for my brother who lives in Virginia, so I need to make sure there's a left and a right shoe and that they're both nine and a half B. I know sometimes mix-ups happen, and two of the same shoe gets in the box, both left or both right shoes. I can't afford any mistakes, because I can't bring them back."

He smiled, saying, "I understand." He checked them and then said, "Yep, a right one, a left one, same size, you're all set. Do you want them gift wrapped?"

As he asked that, I began to think of a neat way to present them to Jimmy. I would borrow a box from my daughter that came from a well-known women's lingerie store. He'd never guess what was in *that* box.

A day or so later, I returned home with my prize. I had his wingtips, and Christmas was going to be wonderful.

I started thinking back to when Jimmy and I were children and how he had always taken care of his little sister. I remembered when I was in first grade and he was in second. My teacher would not excuse me from class to use the bathroom, and I had wet my panties. I was so embarrassed that I wanted to die. I stood out on the playground, tears flowing and kids laughing at me. I felt so ashamed.

Then I heard my name, it was my brother calling me. His class was in the farther part of the playground, and from that distance, he had seen me. He quit playing, came to my part of the yard, grabbed me and hugged me, and wiped my face with his shirt. Then he said, "Come on, I'll take you home."

We lived a couple of miles away. Here we were, a first grader and a second grader, holding hands walking down the sidewalk. He couldn't stand to see me embarrassed and hurt, so he rescued me. He got into trouble for that too.

Jimmy, did I ever thank you for doing that? I don't remember telling you.

As the sweetness of that memory swirled in my mind, I remembered when our family went through a tornado that ripped through our town. I was only ten; Jimmy was barely twelve. We had never seen a tornado, but we got an education that day that we wouldn't have asked for. We saw homes destroyed, people killed, and for the first time in my young life, I experienced sheer terror. My world had been shaken. From that day on, anytime a storm approached, fear overwhelmed me; I was too frightened to be alone.

I would be lying in my bed hearing the storm, scared to breathe, the room dark. Then I'd hear my brother come into my room. He would lay his pillow on the hard floor, lie down on the floor, and reach up for my hand, holding on until the storm passed by. Did I ever say thank you for that, Jimmy?

As I was remembering these things, warm tears rolled down my cheeks. It was as if time and space didn't exist. I was being given a gift, the chance to say thank you to my brother for all the times that he was there meeting a need in *my* life. Now it was my turn. Thank you, Lord, for bringing this together.

A new, exciting idea was being birthed in my heart. I thought of something else I could do as I prayed, "Lord, the shoes are wonderful. They'll meet a physical need for him, but I want to help meet his emotional and spiritual needs too." Jimmy had been so discouraged; he needed to know he *had* made a difference in this world, not only to me, but to many others as well. I picked up the phone and called Jimmy's pastor in Virginia. After identifying myself and exchanging pleasantries, as we had previously met, I told him of our plans for Christmas. He said that Jimmy had shared with him that our entire family would be getting together for the holiday, that he thought it would be so good for Jimmy to be with his family, and that he'd been quite concerned about him. I told him my idea and solicited his help. I asked, "Have you seen the movie *It's a Wonderful Life?*"

"Yeah, great movie."

"Well, remember how all of his friends came to help him when they found out how bad things were?"

"Yes."

"That's what I want to do for Jimmy at Christmas. Would you be willing to contact all of his friends and those he's helped over the years, and anyone else you can think of that loves him, and ask them to write Jimmy a letter telling him what he's meant to them? You can have them mail the letters to me at my parents' home in Georgia so I can present them to my brother on Christmas morning. I want him to know, more importantly, the Lord wants him to know that he *has* made a difference and that the world is a better place because he was born."

We agreed to do it as quietly and discreetly as possible to not spoil the surprise. The pastor thanked me for letting him be a part of the surprise. He and Jimmy were best friends, so he was *really* glad to help.

The time arrived to leave for Georgia. I packed the shoes in the lingerie box, knowing it would add a touch of humor to the unveiling. We left on December 21, arriving on the twenty-second. Jimmy and his family didn't arrive until the twenty-third.

I asked my mom if letters from Virginia had arrived for me, but she said that they hadn't. I was growing nervous.

Would they get there before Christmas? We only had one day left for them to come. Did anyone from Virginia even write one?

All family had arrived by Christmas Eve, and we were visiting when the phone rang. My dad answered it and called me to the phone, saying, "Patty, it's for you."

I said hello; then a man and woman, identifying themselves as calling from Virginia, asked if their letters had arrived. I told them they hadn't and asked how many letters were coming. They said, "Twelve to fourteen that we know of."

I was overjoyed at the response. They began telling me of their love and appreciation for Jimmy and how he'd always reached out to help them, giving not only of his time but also had helped them financially when needed. They thanked me for giving them the opportunity to do this, apologizing that they hadn't thought of doing this themselves. I assured them that it was okay and that I too had failed to say thank you when he'd helped me.

I went back to continue visiting with everyone.

Suddenly, my dad looked at my brother and said, "Jimmy, you *do* still wear a nine-and-a-half B shoe, don't you?"

My heart skipped a beat. I thought Dad was going to let the proverbial cat out of the bag. Jimmy replied, "No, Dad, I don't. My feet have widened, and *now* I wear a nine and a half D. Why do you want to know that?"

"No reason, just wondered," Dad said.

Well, I was sitting there dying a thousand deaths. First, the letters weren't going to get there in time, and now the shoes weren't going to fit.

Looking at my husband, I whispered, "They're not going to fit."

Patting me, he whispered back, "It's okay. It's the thought that counts."

"But he can't wear a thought!"

I went to my room to be alone. What was I going to do?

Sitting in the quiet, I asked God to help me, as nothing seemed to be working out. God's presence was so evident in the room, and I felt as if He spoke to my heart, *Write your own letter to Jimmy. Tell him the thank yous you've always wanted to say.* Taking pen in hand, I began to write, *How do I love you? Let me count the ways.* I began thanking him one-by-one for all the things he'd done for me over the years, recounting and recalling each detail, knowing that as he read he would be taken back to a wonderful time in our lives. It flowed easily from my grateful heart.

Why hadn't I taken the time to say this before? Why hadn't I told him how special he was to me and that I'd always looked up to him with awe, admiration, and respect? Even now, when things were so hard for him, I admired the way he was handling his circumstances with his faith in Christ intact. How thankful I was to the Lord that we both knew as our Savior for giving me the desire of my heart, to share this with my precious brother.

I signed it, sealed it, all was ready for Christmas morning.

We rose early. There were no little ones this year, but adults can get pretty excited over gifts too. After making a pot of coffee and traditional coffee cake and letting the smell drift through the house, beckoning us, we gathered in the living room around the tree.

Anticipation filled my heart. I was so excited! The only thing that could've made it better was for the shoes to fit, but I knew God would make a way, somehow. I began to have a peace settle on me, getting caught up in the celebration of our Lord's birth.

My dad, who plays Santa Claus, started giving out the gifts. I had put my letter on the tree, and it caught Dad's eye. Seeing Jimmy's name on it, he handed it to him. Jimmy opened it, and unfolding the letter, he began to read silently. Others were opening their gifts, but I was watching my gift, unfolding, my eyes fixed on Jimmy. His eyes began to fill, and raising his head, he looked at me with such love. I knew at that instant that God had embraced Jimmy's heart with my words, my thank yous to him. Jimmy came over to me and hugged me, saying, "You're welcome, and I love you too."

My thank yous had been warmly received, but the best was yet to come.

As we all took turns opening our gifts, it was Jimmy's turn to open one of his. Dad handed him a box. I strained to see if it was *the gift*—it was; I was excited and nervous.

So they don't fit, I thought. *I'll figure out some way to exchange them.* As he tore off the outside paper, he noticed the tag that said it was from me, and the name of the lingerie store was revealed, Victoria's Secret. He said, "I can't wait to see what I got from this women's store."

We all laughed making comments. I was thinking, *Will you please hurry up? I'm dying over here!* He cautiously opened the box, hoping nothing would jump out, no doubt. He saw the shoes, and he looked over at me, saying, "Patty, what have you gone and done?" No one else in that room but Jimmy and I knew the significance of the shoes.

As he was taking them out of the box, I said, "Jimmy, you need to know they're the wrong size. I'm sorry, but I bought nine and a half B because we thought that's what you wore."

He got up and kissed me again, saying, "It doesn't matter, Sis; it's what they mean that counts."

The presents continued to be opened; however, I was lost in that special moment and wanted to remain there a little longer, so I kept watching Jimmy and Jeanette as they were admiring the shoes. He put one on the floor and began to try to put his foot into it, and it slipped right in. "Hey, this fits."

Surprised, I said, "It does?"

He took the other shoe out of the box and looked inside it, saying, "Patty, these *are* nine and a half D, the size I wear now."

"What? You're kidding!" I ran over and looked; they *were* nine and a half D. I was in awe. I knew somehow God had intervened in that shoe store to see His expression of love between a brother and sister accomplished.

Days after we arrived back home, I experienced the memory all over again in an even more special way. I was fixing my hair and talking to the Lord in my heart, trying to find some logical explanation. I remembered how many times I had said nine and a half *B* to that shoe salesman, enunciating the *B* so it wouldn't sound like a *D*. As I was pondering this, I felt the Lord bring to my thoughts, *Every time you said B, I made him hear D*. Warm tears of joy ran down my face as I thanked Him once again for His love to us.

You might like to know that the letters from Virginia did come for Jimmy. They arrived the day after Christmas while we were still there. Jimmy went into the bedroom to be alone to read them, I'm sure to cherish each one. He came out of that room a changed man; he knew he *had* made a difference in this world. He knew he had a Lord who loved him enough to bring all of this about. What a Christmas we had, not soon forgotten.

We all realized on that special Christmas that not only God's angels have wings. Wingtip shoes took on a whole new meaning—a fantastic snapshot of grace.

A few years later while speaking in Virginia and staying in my brother's home, I noticed the absence of Jimmy's treasured vintage guitar, one he had gotten as a gift while in the Air Force and had so enjoyed playing over the years. I questioned him as to the whereabouts of his guitar, which was always displayed on a stand in their living room, and he told me he had sold it. I couldn't believe what I was hearing.

"Why would you sell something you loved so much?" I asked.

He paused a few moments then smiled at me and said, "You remember that Christmas when you gave me the wingtip shoes?"

"Yes."

"Well, we wanted to make the trip to Georgia, but money was so tight I didn't think we could afford to go, yet I didn't want to miss out being with everyone. So after a lot of soul-searching, I decided to sell my guitar. I didn't want to, but I knew it was what needed to be done."

I told him I couldn't believe he had had to do that. I was so sad for him. Then I asked, "Jimmy, do you mind telling me how much you sold it for?"

"I took it to a store that specialized in sales of vintage guitars, and he offered me $400 for it, saying he knew it was worth a lot more than that but that was the best he could do. I took the $400 so we could make the trip to see all of you. The guy at the store couldn't believe I would settle for that amount and told me that the guitar was worth way more than what he could give me. I told him I needed the money quickly for something special, and for sure, that Christmas was something very special."

After searching the Internet trying to find Jimmy's guitar to see if I could get it back for him, I discovered that the Gibson B45 series guitars like Jimmy's are worth thousands now, so replacing it wasn't going to happen. A bittersweet reality for me. But our Lord had provided a way for us to be together that Christmas, and no sacrifice was too small to make it happen. Jimmy is without his guitar but still filled with the music of a grateful heart.

Our trust in the Lord and each other deepened. Our faith was renewed that God, indeed, will make a way.

A wonderful ending...

My brother found a great job where he can help people by the work he does, one even better than the job from which he was downsized. They have their beautiful home, and he and his family continue to grow in their love for their Lord, their family, and their friends. They discovered it *is* a wonderful life.

> How much more will your Father which is in heaven give good things to Him that ask Him?
>
> Matthew 7:11b (KJV)

> But seek ye first the kingdom of God and His righteousness, and all these things shall be added unto you.
>
> Matthew 6:33 (KJV)

The Fishing Dream

> Come along with Me and I will show you how to fish for the souls of men.
>
> Matthew 4:19 (TLB)

I had gotten a good night's sleep, yet while I was preparing breakfast, I started remembering a dream. I don't know what spurred the memory of it, but it was coming in bits and pieces. By the end of breakfast it had all fallen into place in my mind. I told my husband before he left for work, "I sure had a strange, even funny, dream last night. I'm just remembering it."

"What was it about?"

"Well, our house was up on stilts, kind of like some beach homes in Florida. In our living room there was a huge hole, an opening, and you could see water. All the furniture was around the edges against the wall around the opening. There was a fishing pole leaning against the wall. In the dream, I was walking around the edge looking down into the water. I picked up the fishing pole and dropped the hook into the water to fish, *in my living room.*"

Spencer said, "Wild dream, but you do love to fish."

"That's not all. Let me tell you the rest. As I was dropping the hook into the water, I noticed there was no bait on the hook, and I thought, *Well, I won't catch anything without bait.* Just as I was finishing that thought, I felt a tug on my pole. I had something on the hook. I pulled it up, and there was a fish on the hook, but it was in a baggie, yes, a baggie. The fish had been cleaned and it was ready for the freezer. I remember thinking, *Well, I didn't have to do a thing. All I did was put the hook out there and everything else was already done.*"

Spencer chuckled after listening, kissed me goodbye, and left for work.

A few days later, I was traveling with some friends from a Bible study group. We were driving to Wichita to attend a Gaither concert. As we were visiting about a lot of different subjects, I decided to use this time together to get a Christian perspective on my crazy dream. I began relating it to the husband and wife I was sharing the backseat with, not realizing that the gentleman driving was also listening to my story.

As I finished, I asked, "Do y'all have an inclination of what that dream means?"

The man driving said, "Patty, I think I know what it means. If you don't get a good witness of agreement in your spirit, then just ignore what I'm telling you, okay?"

"All right," I responded, "go ahead and give me your thoughts."

"I believe the Lord was showing you that He's going to make you a fisher of man's souls, man meaning mankind, just as Christ told Peter and the other disciples in the Bible, some who were fishermen by trade, that He would make them fishers of men. Additionally, you don't need to put bait on the hook because God prepares the hearts; He cleans the hearts, which He showed you that the fish had been cleaned, as He'd done the preparing and the cleaning. The fish in the baggie represented that they were ready to be stored, just as hearts who have accepted Christ are ready to have their names stored in the Lamb's Book of Life. All He needs from you is your willingness to put the hook out there, telling others about Christ."

As the words were being said, I knew that was exactly right. I got a tremendous true witness in my spirit.

Several weeks after our trip, I was invited to speak at my very first Christian Women's Club luncheon in Hutchinson, Kansas. At the end of my talk, giving testimony of my life before knowing Christ and my life after accepting Him, I gave the opportunity for people to pray to accept Him as their Savior and give their lives back to Him. Eight people responded. I was blessed beyond belief. God was confirming to me that He indeed was making me a fisher of souls. The oldest person was eighty-seven years old, and the youngest was fifteen years old, both securing their eternity that day.

There is nothing in this world that compares to that feeling of being a part of someone finding life through accepting Christ, nothing like it, anywhere. It's a burning passion in me to bring others to this relationship, and God provided me the opportunity through Stonecroft Ministries, who sponsored these Christian Women's Clubs across the United States and in many foreign countries. So I have gratefully been a part of that ministry now for some seventeen years, having spoken and sung in over forty states.

God has also provided me opportunities in everyday occurrences, as you've read in other chapters. Another I'd like to share with you wasn't in a planned meeting but was on a plane trip to Georgia.

The two-hour flight from Tulsa to Atlanta was smooth and uneventful; however, the twenty-minute flight from Atlanta to Macon, Georgia, was far from uneventful.

I had boarded the small, nineteen-seat commuter plane and was settling into my usually requested window seat. A very attractive professional-looking woman sat down next to me in the aisle seat. I started to speak to her, but she immediately turned away, speaking to someone a row back on the opposite side. So basically I only saw her from the back, as she remained in that position until we took off.

While she was turned, I noticed her hair was perfectly groomed, her clothes were gorgeous, obviously expensive, and she had long, beautiful, dark red fingernails. I had a bit of envy for the fingernails, I admit.

As the flight attendant came by, she asked my seatmate to please sit straight in her seat for takeoff and to buckle her seat belt, which she hadn't done as yet. This woman sitting next to me never once looked at me or acknowledged that I was even there, so I was feeling a little intimidated as I sat there in my Kmart pantsuit.

The plane took off, and as we were climbing we suddenly hit crosswinds, I assume. The plane tipped violently to the right, throwing my head up against the window and my seatmate against me. There were many screams, including hers. Then the pilot trying to right the aircraft seemed to overcorrect, and we went violently to the left. It was a wild few moments. The plane was finally under control.

People were somewhat in shock, and we all tried to get hold of our emotions.

I started to check myself over to see if I'd been hurt in any way. I experienced a sharp, stabbing pain in my left arm, which was resting on the handle next to my seatmate.

Looking down at my arm, I saw the cause of my stabbing pain. She had those long, red, fingernails dug deeply into my arm. I was staring at it, trying to decide what I should do or say.

She spoke, "My gosh, that was scary. I thought we were going to crash, didn't you?"

"Yes," I said. "It crossed my mind for sure."

"I'm sorry I fell against you and knocked you into the window. Do you hurt anywhere?"

"You couldn't help being thrown into me. I'm okay, except for the pain in my arm." I diverted my eyes to my left arm that was *still* in the grip of those very long fingernails. She looked down to see where I was looking.

Then she saw it. "Oh, I'm so sorry my fingernails are dug into your arm," she said, *still* not letting go.

At this point I gave her a slight grin through my pain, saying, "Whenever you're ready to let go is fine."

She let go quickly, saying, "Oh my gosh, I can't believe I didn't let loose. Did I hurt you?"

I chuckled. "No, I'm fine; don't pay any attention to the blood." I laughed harder to let her know that I was kidding.

She seemed to relax then hesitated a little and said, "Wasn't that the scariest thing you've ever experienced?"

"Yes, it was *very* scary."

She said, "You didn't seem scared at all."

"Well, I *was* scared, but if it was my time, I was ready to go."

"I guess that's the difference between us; you're ready, and I'm not. I noticed the cross on your lapel when I sat down, with the words *Jesus First*. That's why you're ready, isn't it?"

I was surprised by her question because I *never* saw her look at me, much less see a small pin on my lapel.

"To answer your question," I began, "yes, that *is* why I'm ready. My life is in the Lord's hands. We all have an appointed time, I believe, and I don't want to go one minute before my time or stay one minute longer than my time. I know where I'm going, so I do have a peace about it. Do you want to be ready?"

Looking at me, she said, "I've done the blackest of sins."

Since the flight was only twenty minutes, I knew I had to get to the point. "You know what? When Christ died on the cross for our sins, He didn't distinguish colors of sin. His shed blood covers *all* sins."

"Do you really think that is true?"

"Yes, I do. I would stake my life on it."

"How does one go about making sure they are ready if they decide to do that?"

"I'll keep it simple. You just say to God, out loud, or in your heart, 'God, please forgive me for the way I have lived my life. I want your Son as my Savior. Thank you for making me Yours. Amen.'"

We had a smooth landing as we were finishing our conversation.

Distracted by the task of gathering our belongings to deplane, we were both busily preparing to leave. As she got up to leave, she stopped and took a step back to where I was sitting. "Thank you," she said, smiling at me.

"You're very welcome."

I don't know if she ever prayed that prayer, but deep down I have a feeling she did, especially before she flew again.

I *love* fishing, more than ever!

> Don't hide your light! Let it shine for all.
>
> Matthew 5:16a (TLB)

Do You Remember Me?

> What is faith? It is the confident assurance that something we want is going to happen. It is the certainty that what we hope for is waiting for us, even though we cannot see it up ahead.
>
> Hebrews 11:1 (TLB)

When I walked into the room, the meeting was just getting started. Twenty or so mingled around looking for seats. I loved these training sessions on reflective listening. Three to four weeks, meeting on Monday nights, were a valuable part of becoming a volunteer for Helpline, an information/listening service.

My favorite session, without a doubt, was the reflective listening course. I first took the class to become a volunteer on the phone line; then, after several years, I helped teach the classes.

Reflective listening made me a better listener to my husband, my children, my friends, and most importantly, to God. As the word denotes, *reflective* means to reflect back to others what you heard them say.

I remember the first exercise we were asked to do during my first class. We were paired in twos. Chairs were positioned back to back. The man I partnered with took his seat, as did I. We were now sitting back to back, so naturally we couldn't see each other. We were instructed to take turns talking, five minutes each, telling something about ourselves. Then the other person was supposed to tell what they thought *they* heard. The man went first telling me about himself, and then it was my turn to say what I'd heard him say.

I'd always thought I was a good listener, but I quickly found out that I was sorely lacking. I realized as I began to say what I had heard that I actually only heard the first few sentences of his talk. I found that as I listened to him I began thinking about what I was going to say in my five minutes and discovered that you can't really hear another person while you're thinking about other things. We all do it without realizing it. We can't wait to talk. We're creating, editing, and organizing our thoughts, all while someone is giving us important information. That was a real eye-opener for me.

Training to be a volunteer to answer calls on Helpline was both a challenge and a blessing. I had to learn to listen to people I could not see and did not know. No body language or facial expressions to watch, just a voice on the other end of the phone. I was taught to train my ear to hear, really hear, what the caller was saying or not saying. While Helpline was mostly an information source, some calls were of a crisis nature, so the training to talk someone through situations was imperative.

Everyone had settled into their seats. I and another woman would be leading the exercise that night. We chose three people from around the table to give one sentence about themselves.

The three shared, then we, as the facilitators, were to pick one from the three to hear more from that person, then reflect back to them what we'd heard them say. Two had interesting sentences; the third was monotone and boring. I chose her.

The other teacher with me asked quietly why I'd chosen the one that really had nothing to say. I told her that I heard something in this woman's intonation that drew my attention. The other facilitator said for me to go ahead and do the reflective listening exercise with the woman.

Her monotone and boring sentence went something like this, "My husband is away in France. My daughter and I are going out for dinner tonight." Nothing there, it seemed.

As I asked her to share more about herself, she talked a little while longer. Then it was my turn to reflect back what I'd understood her to say. So I began, repeating to her and the others what I'd heard. She nodded in agreement that I had accurately heard her words. I then began to reflect on the *emotions* I had heard.

"Do I hear sadness in your voice?" I asked.

"Yes."

"Do I hear a kind of desperation, a giving up tone to your words?"

She nodded yes.

The room went dead silent. God was giving me insight into this woman's heart. Here I was in a worldly setting, not a religious gathering, and God was teaching me that He wants to help me in *all* situations. He tells us in the Bible, if we lack wisdom, we have only to ask, and He'll give wisdom.

He revealed to me a desperate soul.

I stopped the exercise and asked her if she wanted to go out of the room with me to talk privately. She said yes, she wanted to do that. We excused ourselves and went out into the hall.

I began by asking her name.

"Chip."

"Is that your real name or a nickname?"

"A nickname, but that's the only name I like."

"Okay, Chip it is. My name is Patty."

"How did you know I was desperate and ready to give up?"

Looking at her intently, I said, "God showed that to me."

"*God?* I'm an atheist; I don't *believe* in God!" she stated strongly.

"Okay, let me ask you this, and tell me if I'm wrong. Do you have plans to take your life?"

Her mouth dropped open, "How did you know that?" She started crying as if a deep, dark, shameful secret had been revealed.

"Chip, God told me that while I was listening to you in the meeting."

"That can't be true," she said. "No one knows what I've been planning."

"Then you *were* planning to do something?"

"Yes, I've been accumulating pills to take all at once, when I had enough," she answered angrily.

"Chip, listen to me, God loves you. It doesn't matter right now if you believe in Him or not. What *does* matter is that He loved you enough to tell someone so you wouldn't take your life. He wants you to live."

She was crying louder now. I put my arms around her. "Would you be willing to meet with me so we can talk some more? I believe we can work through this together." She nodded yes. "Chip, will you promise me that you won't go through with your plans?"

"For right now," she answered.

Over the next several months we met at her home and talked. We formed a great bond of friendship and respect. God always gave me insight as to what to say, and it seemed to be just what she needed to hear that day. I always gave credit to God for the insight, but she continued to reject the thought of God. She told me she'd been to a professional counselor earlier, but it hadn't helped her. They had not really heard her, she felt.

During these months, she began showing up at my concerts with her husband and daughter. I thought it strange for someone who professed not to believe in God to come to listen to music and testimony about nothing but God.

At the end of my concerts, I gave the opportunity for people to come forward to accept Christ as their Savior. Chip never came forward.

After many months, I saw positive changes in her demeanor and attitude. She was definitely better and was hopeful about life in general. After a time, our lives took different paths, and I lost track of Chip.

Over the years God would bring Chip to my mind, and I would pray for her, always wondering where life had taken her and her family.

It was a nice drive to Kansas, where I had been invited to speak at the Christian Women's Club. As I went in I had to quickly get my mind together, as it was almost time for me to speak.

The women were visiting before the meeting started, so I went to my seat at the head table, said my hellos and thanks for having me, then began to take a moment to review my notes.

My head was down as I was reading. I heard someone clear their throat rather loudly, as if seeking my attention. I looked up to see a woman standing on the opposite side of my table. She said, "Do you remember me?"

I couldn't believe my eyes. "Of course I remember you, Chip." She grinned at my recognition of her. "How wonderful to see you. What in the world are you doing in Olathe, Kansas?"

"We live here. My husband retired, and we bought a farm. He'd always wanted to farm. I saw your picture in the paper and that you were speaking here today, so

I had to come hear you. You're going to sing too, aren't you?"

"Yes, I sure am. How long has it been since I've seen you? I lost track of you. Someone told me you had moved, but they weren't sure to where."

"Nineteen years. It's been nineteen years," she answered.

"Wow. Well, we both still look good, don't we?" We laughed.

"So what kind of meeting is this?"

"Well," I explained, "it's a Christian Women's Club. I speak and sing for their organization all over the United States. I give my testimony, so that's what you'll hear today. I'm so glad you're here. What a great surprise."

The meeting started, so Chip went back to her seat. At the close of the meeting, I gave the opportunity for those who wanted to receive Christ as their Savior to pray the prayer of salvation with me, silently. Cards were passed out, and I asked that those who had prayed the prayer to indicate their decision on the card, giving it to me after the meeting.

Approaching me, card in hand, Chip gave me her card, saying, "Look what I've done today, Patty. I asked Jesus to be my Savior. God *is* real."

What an awesome God, I thought. I could hardly contain myself. I grabbed her, giving her a big hug. It was a great moment—a snapshot of grace for sure, something to be treasured. Nineteen years had passed. Nineteen years I had prayed for her as God brought her to my mind. God had graciously let me be a part of the planting of the seed in her life in that reflective listening class so many years ago, a part of the watering over the years with my prayers, along with many others, I'm sure. Thankfully, He let me be a part of the reaping of her soul for His glory. Hallelujah!

Her name is now written in the Lamb's Book of Life. Her name, a name remembered, *Chip*. How awesome is that?

> He is the God who keeps every promise. He opens the eyes of the blind; He lifts the burdens from those bent down beneath their loads.
>
> Psalm 146:6, 8 (TLB)

> He heals the brokenhearted and binds up their wounds.
>
> Psalm 147:3 (TLB)

Our Isaac

And when you draw close to God, God will draw close to you.

James 4:8 (TLB)

Beareth all things, believeth all things, hopeth all things, endureth all things

1 Corinthians 13:7 (KJV)

August 7, 1982, was a typical warm, summer day.

On August 6, I had been asked to sing at a women's meeting. The speaker was a pastor's wife. Her talk was wonderful. She spoke of how God had healed her of a blood disorder that had plagued her for several years. Doctors had little success in treating her. She gave a scripture, among several, during her talk, but this one scripture stuck in my mind. "Behold, I am the Lord, the God of all flesh. Is anything too difficult for Me?" (Jeremiah 32:27 NAS).

I remember as I drove home from the meeting that scripture kept running through my mind. Little did I know that God was writing it on the tablet of my heart for a reason.

The phone call that any parent dreads came at 11:15 p.m. on August 7. Our son, John, was in the emergency room. He was due home by 11:00 p.m., but now the nurse on the phone was telling me he'd been injured and we needed to come as quickly as possible. We had received several of these phone calls before, when John had car accidents over the last couple of years. Thinking this was also a car accident, I asked the nurse, "Was he injured in an automobile accident?"

"No."

"So how was he injured? What happened to him?"

She hesitated and said, "Mrs. Curl, your son has been shot."

I remember hearing someone scream. It was me. "Oh my God. No, no. How? What happened?"

"Ma'am, we don't know any of the circumstances. We just know he's been shot. He's in grave condition."

It seemed the call went on for a long time, but actually, it was only seconds as I told her through sobs and screams we were on our way.

We live twenty minutes from town. Already in pajamas for the night, I went to wake my husband for us to hurry and dress. Our daughter, Lori, was on a date and due home any minute. She was recovering from a car accident about a month earlier. An elderly man had hit her car broadside as she was coming home from her job. She had a broken arm and facial lacerations but was healing well, thankfully.

Spencer was in a daze, trying to understand how this happened. Getting his senses together, he began throwing on clothes. As we were ready to leave, Lori and her date drove up. I tried to calm myself to tell her. She wept uncontrollably, as expected, not understanding how this could have happened to her brother. It felt like we were all moving in slow motion.

Just that afternoon, John had asked if he and a friend could go frog-gigging. We told him he could but to be home by 11:00 p.m. Off they went, in old T-shirts, cutoff shorts, tennis shoes, and frog-gigging spears for a day of fun at the lake. John loved fried frog legs.

A few days earlier, on June 30, John had just celebrated his seventeenth birthday. Now he was fighting for his life.

Arriving at the hospital, we couldn't get inside fast enough. Prayers were on my lips as I silently prayed, *God, help us. I don't want to lose my boy.* I pled for his life.

We stepped into the entrance of the ER.

Lining the walls of the entrance were a lot of people from my church, holding hands and praying. I was overwhelmed with gratitude. I had called the church prayer chain before leaving the house, screaming into the phone, "This is Patty Curl. Our son, John, is in the ER. He's been shot. Please call people to pray." These people not only prayed; they came to be with us to give their love and support.

As we passed the prayer warriors, they reached out and patted us. We stepped to the ER window and gave our name. We were told a doctor would come out to talk to us in a few minutes. It seemed like an eternity.

The ER doctor took us aside, telling us that John was very critical and that they'd requested a medi-flight helicopter to transport John to a brain trauma hospital in Tulsa, two hours away by car, forty-five minutes by air. The doctor explained that the bullet had entered the brain, he believed, through John's face. When I heard John had been shot in the face, I almost fainted. The doctor continued telling us that they couldn't stabilize his vitals, his blood pressure, especially, and stated that he couldn't be transported *until* he was stable and that his survival was looking dim.

All of this was so hard for us to process. We were clinging to hope, certainly more prayer required.

It's hard to describe the gut-wrenching emotions. You're moving in a fog, mind and body. I looked at Spencer, white as a sheet, traumatized, both of us not sure of anything. I said, "Honey, go in and see John. I need to prepare myself for a minute." I didn't know how I would handle seeing my boy near death. "I'll be right behind you."

I walked over to those who were praying. My pastor was among them. I asked, "Please pray for John to stabilize so they can put him on the helicopter for Tulsa."

I followed Spencer into where our son lay. "God, please save him," I whispered. Looking at him, I couldn't breathe.

He was gray. His body was still and lifeless.

Tubes and machines were everywhere, in and around his body.

There was no movement.

His face so twisted and swollen from the trauma that the right side of his face was almost unrecognizable.

He didn't look like John, but I knew it was. I recognized the clothes he was wearing when he left our house.

We reached out to touch him. I leaned down with my tears dripping on him, gently kissing first his hand, then his forehead, his left cheek, and lastly, the mutilated right side. As I kissed him, I remembered when he was a little boy and he would fall down and come in crying, "Mama, kiss it and make it all better." If only, I could.

Back in the waiting room watching for the helicopter to arrive, I saw my pastor talking to a young man in handcuffs. I noticed a lot of teenagers standing in the waiting area. As I walked among them, the smell of alcohol was overwhelming. I asked why they were there, and one of the girls told me they'd all been out at the lake when John got shot.

I saw a police officer and asked if I could speak to him. I started asking rapid-fire questions. "Do you know what happened? Why is that man in handcuffs?" The officer asked who I was. I told him that I was the mother of the boy who'd been shot.

"First, ma'am, let me say how sorry I am about your son. We're still piecing together what exactly happened, but we do believe the young man in cuffs shot your son. The circumstances may have been accidental, but we're still gathering information. The man *is* very intoxicated, but several here have pointed him out as the one with the rifle."

After that conversation, I walked up to the man in handcuffs, who was facing the wall. I tapped him on the shoulder, and he turned to look at me. He was sweaty, dirty, and reeked of alcohol. My heart wanted to hate him, but I knew if I wanted my prayers answered I *had* to forgive, no matter what. In the Bible, Jesus said, "And whenever you stand praying, forgive if you have anything against anyone so that your Father also who is in heaven may forgive your transgressions. But if you do not forgive, neither will your Father forgive your transgressions" (Mark 11:25, 26 KJV).

I was looking into eyes that were clearly out of focus, red from crying, and looking past me. I wanted him to hear me, so I put my hand on his chin. "Son," I began, "I don't know why you did what you did, but I want to tell you I'm the mother of the boy you shot. Do you understand that? I'm his mother."

He nodded yes.

"I want you to know…" I continued as he slowly started turning his head away. "Please look me in the eyes." His eyes locked onto mine. "What I want you to know is this; even though I don't understand why, I forgive you."

He started sobbing loudly then asked me, "How can you forgive me?"

I stared for moments at this pathetic person in front of me and said, "Because, I am a Christian, and if I want *my* prayers answered for my son's life, I need to forgive you. So I choose to forgive."

I walked away, leaving him bewildered, no doubt questioning, and hopefully seeking that forgiveness for himself. I asked my pastor to please go to the jail and minister to him.

Spencer, Lori, and I were surrounded by those who had come to pray and give comfort as we waited. We joined hands and prayed. After that, my pastor, David Satterfield, told us he was going into the ER room to pray for John before going to the jail. We continued to wait, hope, and pray.

The helicopter landed in the parking lot of the hospital. The ER team told us that John's vitals had stabilized enough for the flight to Tulsa and that John was moving his arms and legs, a hopeful sign. God had heard the prayers. The doctors feared paralysis with the brain injury, which was still a possibility, but hope wouldn't leave us. We clung tightly to it.

They whisked John past us on the way out to load him on the helicopter. I could see him flailing about, but he still wasn't conscious. I ran alongside to board with him. The medical staff wouldn't let me get on, explaining there wasn't enough room for me, only room for those taking care of John. I pleaded with them, to no avail. I was devastated. I didn't know if I'd ever see him alive again. I wanted to be with him.

Spencer grabbed me in a hug to support me. I was crumbling inside.

We watched the helicopter ascend into the blackness with our precious, broken son.

The three of us gathered ourselves to make the two-hour drive to Tulsa. It was now about 1:30 a.m.

Spencer said, "We need to get cash. I've got to go to the ATM. We don't know how long we'll be in Tulsa. We'll need a motel, food, and gas. I'll take you home to pack our clothes; then we'll head out to Tulsa." Lori followed us home in her boyfriend's car.

Back at the house, Lori helped me pack while waiting for her boyfriend to return. He had offered to drive her to Tulsa. We were both frozen with fear and trying to make sense of a senseless tragedy. I think at that point I was running on autopilot. The fog had definitely thickened in my mind. I just couldn't believe this was really happening. Lori kept me sane and focused, helping me think of what I really needed to take. I remember telling her that I needed to pack clothes for John so he'd have something to wear home. A weak effort at faith, I'm afraid.

Walking into his room, I grabbed a shirt from his closet. He'd worn it that morning before he went to the lake. Holding it up to my face, I found it smelled of John. I breathed in the essence of my son. I cried into the shirt, burying my face into it as I prayed, "Lord, I need Your peace. I don't know if John's going to live or die. Be with us; walk us through this dark valley." As I prayed those last words, *dark valley,* I slid off the bed onto my knees, and I began to pray the Twenty-third Psalm.

> The Lord is my shepherd I shall not want, He makes me to lie down in green pastures. He leads me beside quiet waters, He restores my soul... even though I walk through the valley of the shadow of death, I will fear no evil, for Thou art with me, Thy rod and Thy staff they comfort me.
>
> Psalm 23:1–3, 4 (NAS)

I drew strength from those words written more than two thousand years ago but alive for today.

The drive to Tulsa seemed to take forever, but looking back, I know God needed the time to minister to

Spencer and me in a personal way to prepare us for the days ahead.

Silence was the third passenger in the car. I can't tell you what Spencer was thinking or feeling during that drive; we've never spoken of it. But I will tell you my story, though painfully glorious to relive yet one that needs to be told to the praise of God.

My thoughts were a struggle going on in my spirit. *Lord, just let me know, is he going to live or die?*

I was staring blankly at the windshield, and it was as if a movie screen was displayed on the glass.

I saw Abraham carrying his son, Isaac, up to the mountain to be sacrificed, the story in the Bible in the twenty-second chapter of Genesis. God had asked Abraham if he would sacrifice his son. Abraham loved God and completely trusted Him, and though he didn't want to give up his son, he believed God knew what He was doing and would somehow make it right, which He did. He provided a ram for the sacrifice instead. It was a lesson in trusting.

Still riding in the car, I was continuing to watch Abraham carrying his son as it was playing out in front of me on the windshield.

Then in the silence, I heard whispered in my spirit, *Will you give me John?* No words were coming from my mouth. I was speaking to God in my thoughts. *Lord, take me if You want to take someone.*

He whispered again, *Will you give me your son?* I sat there riveted for a long time, remembering how God had, at the last minute, provided a sacrifice for Abraham. He did not really want Isaac, but could *I* trust Him now?

I thought about how long I had known God personally, through a relationship with His Son, Christ, of how He'd loved me, cared for me, and of my very deep love for Him as my heavenly Father. Speaking once again to Him in my mind, I said, "God, I don't always understand Your ways, and if You take John You'll have to fill a very large hole in my heart. You'll have to care for him until I can be with him again. I know John knows Christ as his Savior, so I know he'll be with You; I do trust You, but it's so hard, Lord."

My heart was about to burst. I swallowed hard. "Lord, I don't understand why, but I know I love You, and I'll have to choose to trust You." I paused to consider my words. "So I," I said, struggling with my choice, "I give ... I'll give You my ... son." I started sobbing quietly, thinking, *Oh my God, what have I done?*

Then the loudest whisper of all came into my ear. *Patty, I promise you from this moment forward your son will be as whole and healthy as the day he was born.*

Oh my God, my God, how wonderful You are! I didn't know how, and I didn't know when, but I knew John was going to live and be whole. The hows and whens were God's business.

I experienced such a shot of faith like I'd never known. I'd had what is called a *Rhema* word given to me—the voice of the Holy Spirit as He speaks to the believer at the present moment—and I knew that I knew it was from God. I was ready for whatever came.

Spencer spoke to me at that moment, sharing thoughts he was wrestling with. It jolted me at first, hearing the silence finally broken. "Why of all the places on his body did John get shot in his brain, the place that controls everything? Why his brain?"

The scripture God had written on my heart just the day before spilled out. "Honey, in Jeremiah 32:27, God said, 'Behold, I am the Lord, the God of all flesh. Is anything too difficult for Me?' Nothing is too hard for God. And just think of the wonderful testimony of God's healing power for it to be John's brain." As the words were out there, I was thinking, *Wow, where has all this faith come from?* Something truly wonderful had happened to me in that car on the way to a Tulsa hospital, a true divine appointment.

Spencer spoke again. "Well, I've decided one thing. I won't allow John to be hooked up to machines to be kept alive. He wouldn't want to live like that, and I won't let that happen."

Looking over at Spencer, I said, "Well, you're not going to have to make that decision because God has just promised me that John is going to be as whole and healthy as the day he was born." He looked at me like I'd lost my bloomin' mind. Then I realized that Spencer didn't know what had gone on with me in those hours of silence in the car. All he knew was what I had just shared that God had promised me. He was a little confused, not surprisingly.

We arrived at the hospital and went by the directions we were given as to John's location there. It was now about 4:00 a.m. We were shown to a waiting room. We were alone with our thoughts and our prayers. Our daughter Lori and her boyfriend joined us as soon as they got to the hospital.

A doctor came in and introduced himself as John's neurosurgeon. He began by telling us John was alive. They had done an MRI, finding that the .22 caliber bullet was lodged in his brain and that it had entered at the top of John's right ear. (He had not been shot in the face as first thought at our local hospital.)

He told us that John's cheekbone was shattered and his nose was broken. His right eye was nearly out of its socket.

He added that he felt that John's facial injuries were caused by him falling face down after being shot. He said they were prepping him for surgery.

Then he began telling us all the things that could happen or go wrong.

He said John might not survive the surgery. He could be brain damaged *if* he lived, and he fully expected paralysis on his left side, explaining the affected right side of the brain controls the left side of the body. He told us John was facing the possible loss of his right eye. He wanted to prepare us that the odds were against him even making it through surgery.

It was like standing at the edge of the ocean. Wave after wave comes, each time knocking you down, you get back up and here comes the next one.

I knew the doctor had to warn us of all the possibilities, but it was so very hard to hear.

Just before leaving, the doctor asked if there was anything we'd like to ask or say. Remembering my divine appointment and God's promise, I jumped in with both feet.

"Doctor," I began, "we're Christians, and there are a lot of prayers going up for John. I believe God has promised me John would live. So I'd like for you to look for miracles, because you're not going into that operating room alone."

He reached over and patted me on the shoulder and said, "Okay, Mrs. Curl." He paused, as if putting aside my request to look for miracles. "The surgery will probably take three, maybe four hours. I'll come and speak with you later."

So it was in God's hands.

One hour and forty-five minutes later, the doctor returned, so the surgery hadn't taken as long as expected. I knew that could be a good thing or a bad thing. I chose to believe it was a good thing.

He started by putting his hand on the same shoulder he had patted earlier. "Well, Mrs. Curl, you have your miracles."

To hear that from a doctor got my attention, especially since he'd seemed skeptical about the miracle thing.

He continued, "Your son has the heart of a lion."

My faith was saying to me, *Yes, the Lion of Judah.*

"The bullet was a .22 caliber, long-rifle bullet, longer than a normal .22 bullet. It stopped one inch short of exiting the skull and is resting in a fissure. Had the bullet exited, it would have left a huge hole and would certainly have killed John, but it didn't exit. So there's one of your miracles.

"Here's another amazing thing, the bullet entered the top right of John's right ear. Its trajectory should have taken it straight across and out of the left side, but for some reason, the bullet made a left turn after entry, ending up on the same right side, at the top back part of his head. Unbelievable. Everything seems to be going right for this young man."

I was smiling the biggest smile ever at the doctor. Confirmation of God's promise rolling out of his mouth brought us hope, joy, and definitely praise for God's hand in this.

He continued to tell us that John wasn't out of the woods and that many negative things could happen. He still expected some paralysis on the left side and told us that John's brain stem had been moved as far as it could be moved and that survival chances are greatly diminished after that kind of drastic movement. Also, he feared that mental and/or motor skills might be severely affected.

We were getting a sense that the bullet hadn't been removed, since he'd not mentioned removal, only telling us where the bullet stopped and its location. So I asked, "Did you leave the bullet in there?"

"That's right. We made the decision that retrieving it from healthy brain tissue wasn't the best course to take."

"But won't the bullet move around? Can't it get infected or do damage?"

"Mrs. Curl, that's one of the most extraordinary things that happened. Where the bullet stopped, resting in the fissure, is the best place it could be. Think of a sponge. You have those indentations. Well, that's where the bullet is. It's tucked into an indentation, a fissure. And this is also extraordinary. When a bullet comes out of a gun, it's spinning rapidly due to the striations in the cylinder (I remember the doctor demonstrating a spiraling motion with his finger). The spinning makes the bullet hot, so when the bullet stopped one inch short of exiting the skull, it tucked into the fissure, and because of the heat, it cauterized all the tissue around it. Cauterization cleanses, so John's chances of infection are probably a million to one. It's as if the bullet was controlled from the moment of entry to do the least amount of damage. Just unbelievable."

He was shaking his head, we were smiling. God is good.

I was thinking at that moment maybe miracles *had* become part of the doctor's thought processes. It could be he experienced a *divine appointment* in that operating room, discovering he wasn't alone in there.

"One last thing," he said. "Where the bullet entered at the top of his right ear, I removed damaged tissue and part of the skull, so there's a hole in the skull about the size of an egg. I thought about putting a steel plate there to protect the area but decided against it, so we'll need to watch that closely.

"You do need to know that John is a very shattered young man and will have a long road to recovery. His eye will require surgery at some point and his broken nose also. So we're optimistic but cautiously optimistic. I do believe his cognitive skills will be greatly diminished, and he'll experience some personality changes due to the brain trauma, but he's alive. You can go see him. He'll be with us a while, I'm sure, and we'll deal with his issues as they arise. Meanwhile, he'll stay in the brain trauma unit."

We thanked the doctor, and I gave him a hug for all he'd done for John.

Spencer, Lori, and I went to John's room after the surgery. He was in a semi-coma, which wasn't uncommon according to the doctor. After hugging him and loving on him, we went to make all of the necessary phone calls to loved ones who were waiting to hear.

The time was around 6:00 a.m., and Lori had to return home to her job and also take care of the house and feed our pets. She had been with us all night, wanting to be sure that her brother was out of surgery and alive before she left. Bless her heart, she was so torn about having to leave, but there was nothing more she could do except pray. So we hugged her as she was leaving. Also, we thanked her boyfriend for driving her to Tulsa. We promised to call every day to update her. As a mother, I was concerned for her well-being since she'd been up all night helping us in so many ways, making phone calls I couldn't make, holding me when I'd start to break down. Just having her there was such a blessing, as all our family needed to be together.

When you are so blessed with God's grace, you feel that you need to pass that on to others. I was given that opportunity.

Anyone who has stayed in a hospital waiting room, especially an ICU waiting room for days, knows you become like family to those literally living there. Everyone is dealing with life and death issues. You're all in the same proverbial boat.

John was having good days and bad days, not unexpected, but a roller coaster nonetheless. I slept in his room after he was moved to the neuro-surgery floor but would go to the ICU waiting area several times during the day to visit families I had become acquainted with.

Spencer had to return to work after spending a few days in Tulsa. Lori had driven to Tulsa again to visit John but needed to return to her job as well, so it was just John, me, and the Lord.

There was a couple I befriended in the ICU waiting area. Their son came in the night after John. He was a motocross racer and had actually won the event. Later that evening, he was in a pickup truck with friends. They crossed a railroad where there were no crossing bars, only a flashing signal, which the boys must not have seen. A train hit their truck. Their son had sustained a serious brain injury and was air lifted to Tulsa.

I'll never forget as doctors would come into the ICU waiting area, each going to different families to update them with good or bad news. We'd watch to see if loved ones were okay. John's doctor walked in one afternoon with the doctor of the motocross boy right behind. Our doctor told me John was definitely going to survive. I took a thankful breath. I heard a loud, "No, no, please," from across the room. Their doctor had told them their son was brain dead, there was no hope, and they'd have to make a decision. The parents were devastated.

After the doctor left, I went over to put my arms around the couple. I couldn't help but feel some guilt that we got to have our son but they were losing theirs. My heart broke for them.

Later that day, as I was getting on the elevator to go to the cafeteria, someone called out as the door was closing, "Hold the door, please." I put my hand out to stop it, and the mom of that boy got on with me. It was just the two of us in the elevator.

We began talking, and I again told her how my heart broke for her about her son and that I'd be praying for them. She thanked me and told me how happy she was that John was going to make it, knowing how serious his injuries were. She then went on to say that she'd noticed this peace about me. Despite the turmoil, I seemed to have peace.

Then she asked, "Where does that come from?"

My chance to share the grace.

"Well, it comes from my relationship with Jesus Christ. I would never have survived this without Him. No matter which way it turned out, I knew He would take care of us. *All* of us."

She looked at me and said, "You know, I used to go to church many years ago; then I just stopped going. I don't know why exactly, but I know now, I feel *very* alone."

"Church *is* important; however, your attendance in church is not what I'm talking about. Having a personal, loving relationship with God and His Son is what I'm talking about."

"How do you get that?" she asked. As the elevator stopped at the next floor, we stepped out to find a quiet, private place to talk. This was a life-changing, divinely inspired moment, no doubt.

I began, "You pray to ask Christ into your heart. You have to believe in your heart He is who He says He is. You give Him your life, to be Lord of it, to make you what He intended you to be when He gave you life. There are so many benefits that follow that prayer. You'll experience a personal, loving relationship, which brings intimacy with the divine and total access to God, a peace like you've never known and such joy for living, comfort through the worst of times, like now, and one of the best benefits, knowing where you're going when you leave this world."

"Could you pray with me now?"

"Absolutely, I'd be honored to."

A few days later, they made the torturous decision to remove life support, letting go, of their son.

I called the Oral Roberts prayer line in Tulsa and asked if they could send someone to be with this couple since they had no family close by. They were from a northern state and had only been in Oklahoma for the motocross race. Within thirty minutes of my phone call, several people arrived from ORU to minister to this family's needs. God's family at work.

A week had passed since John's shooting. Pieces began to fall together about the incident.

The nineteen-year-old had been arrested for reckless use of a firearm. He'd driven to the lake while drinking heavily and shot a rifle at several locations around the lake. He'd stopped in the area where John was frog-gigging and was firing in the air and across the lake. Some men at the lake heard the gunfire and decided to go find who was putting people in danger. They found the man, and an argument ensued as they asked him to leave. There was a struggle for the gun, and the rifle went off. John was standing a few feet away, and the bullet struck him as he watched the fight.

Thirteen days after brain surgery, John was released from the hospital. He had beaten his doctor in a game of chess, and the doctor said, "Obviously, nothing wrong with his mental skills." So he signed him out, with an appointment to see him in six weeks for a follow-up checkup.

God was indeed at work in those thirteen days in the hospital. John did experience paralysis in his left leg, but as the nurse left the room to inform the doctor of the problem, I tried to calm John, as he was understandably upset about the paralysis.

I said, "Honey, just lie back a minute." I put my hand on his left leg and prayed, "Lord, You promised whole and healthy as the day he was born, and we thank You for that." The doctor arrived in a few minutes, looked at the empty bed, and asked, "Where's John?"

I told him John was in the bathroom. He asked, "How did he get to the bathroom? Did you help him get there?"

"No, he walked in there by himself."

John walked out of the bathroom at that moment pushing his IV machine, spoke to the doctor, and got back into bed. The doctor began examining his leg and all his reflexes, which were normal. John said, "Doc, I had a problem with my leg, couldn't feel it or move it, but it's okay now; my mom prayed."

The doctor said, "That's great." With a bewildered smile, he left the room.

God was at work again.

John came home.

Bringing him home was unbelievable. I don't think any of us, including the medical people, thought it would happen that quickly, after only thirteen days.

School had begun, but John had to wait a month to begin his senior year. He had a patch on his right eye and a large scar on the right side of his head, which was shaved and mostly bandaged. He remembered very little of what had happened to him that night. We decided not to discuss it unless he asked, he needed to heal.

One evening, John and I were sitting outside in lawn chairs. The sun had just gone down, so seeing each other was becoming difficult.

John wanted to talk about God.

He began to say he knew how seriously he had been injured. He'd heard the doctors and nurses talking. And he knew God had brought him through. He spoke of how sorry he was that he hadn't paid much attention to his relationship with the Lord for a long time and that he had so much gratitude to God for sparing his life.

As he was talking, I heard a loud *pop,* as if someone had popped all their knuckles at once. "John, what was that?"

"It was my nose; it just popped." He began breathing in and out, in and out. He said excitedly, "Mom, I can breathe completely through my nose. The air isn't restricted anymore."

Whole and healthy as the day he was born.

The doctor's appointment for John's broken nose was the next day after the nose popping incident. It was a follow-up visit to the ENT doctor (ear, nose, and throat). We arrived and were shown to an exam room. We'd seen the ENT doctor a few days after John came home from the hospital and had discussed surgery to repair his nose, as his air intake was severely restricted, especially on the right side, where all the damage had occurred. So that day we were seeing the doctor again to actually schedule the surgery.

The doctor came in, greeted us, and began to examine John's nose. He stepped back and said, "When were you last here?"

"It's been about a week and a half."

He looked at John's medical file and said, "Well, I've written here that I was to repair and straighten his nose, as it was blocked up into the right nostril, but his nose is perfectly aligned. There's nothing for me to fix." John and I smiled at each other, and John then told the doctor what had happened the night before as we were sitting outside, how his nose had just popped all by itself, allowing him to breathe freely. The doctor just said, "Well, that's amazing. I guess we're getting a little help from above."

Looking at him, I said, "No doubt about that."

The next doctor's visit was for John's right eye to have it assessed as to what needed to be done. We had an appointment at Dean McGee Eye Institute, one of the most prestigious eye facilities in the United States and thankfully located in our home state.

After arriving, we had to fill out all necessary paperwork. Many of John's medical records had been forwarded by his Tulsa doctors, so they were aware of John's brain injury and the severity of it. The first eye surgeon came into the room and began to talk with John about what had happened to him. John was vague on many of the questions asked. I filled in the blanks when necessary. He remarked to John, "To think that you had brain surgery only a few weeks ago is amazing.

Son, you shouldn't even be alive." We agreed with him, and he asked if he could invite several more doctors into the room to meet John and discuss not only his injuries but his amazing recovery. John and I consented to the other doctors joining us.

They examined his badly injured eye. The eyeball was sitting in the very right corner of the eye socket, which made his pupil hard to see. They explained that surgery would be required to straighten his eye, snipping the muscle on both sides and reattaching and tightening them to bring the eyeball back to center. However, they wanted to wait at least six months to give John time to heal from his traumatic head injury. They fit John with more substantial eye coverings to replace the patches he'd been wearing. We went home to continue living our lives to return in six months for his eye surgery.

John excelled in school, and we were so thankful, to the glory of God, for his mental skills being intact.

Sometimes God heals supernaturally (without man's participation), or He uses doctors to bring about healing, all for a purpose. Ours is not to ask why, but to trust.

I had questioned why John had to have eye surgery. Why couldn't God touch his eye as He'd touched John's nose?

God, in a gentle way, let me know He'd decide how John's healing would take place. That's as it should be. There's a scripture that addresses that. The Lord said, "Behold, let Me tell you, you are not right in this. For God is greater than man. Why do you complain against Him, that He does not give an account of all

His doings?" (Job 33:12–13 NAS). I considered myself properly told to butt out. God does know what He's doing.

I realized as time went on that God wanted John's healing to be visible to as many people as possible. He wanted doctors to see His grace and power in dealing with His creation, a testimony that God is true to His word and His promises.

John did have his eye surgery. However, after waiting the six months, upon arriving for the surgery, we discovered John's eye had moved toward the center all by itself. Now it was only one-fourth off-center, and the surgery didn't take as long.

The repairs had been made by the Almighty, and God in His goodness allowed the doctors to finish His work.

A promise kept…

Forgiveness was required several times in this story, required for the promises of God to go forth. Even though the man who shot John was charged with reckless use of a firearm while intoxicated, he was sentenced to only one weekend in jail and only a $50 fine. This man had changed the course of my son's life in a very negative way, yet as we heard of the unjust sentence, God required my forgiveness again, which I gave and continue to give.

> For the battle is the Lord's.
>
> 1 Samuel 17:47b

> The Lord is my rock and my fortress and my deliverer. My God, my rock, in whom I take ref-

uge; my shield and the horn of my salvation, my stronghold and my refuge. My savior, Thou dost save me from violence. I call upon the Lord, who is worthy to be praised. And I am saved from my enemies. For the waves of death encompassed me, the torrents of destruction overwhelmed me, the snares of death confronted me. In my distress I called upon the Lord. Yes, I cried out to my God; and from His temple He heard my voice, and my cry for help came into His ears. Then the earth shook and quaked, the foundations of heaven were trembling and were shaken because He was angry. He bowed the heavens also, and came down. He delivered me from my strong enemy. From those who hated me, for they were too strong for me, but the Lord was my support, He rescued me.

2 Samuel 22:2–4, 7, 8, 10b, 18, 19b, 20b

Another part of this story should be told, for when God works, He goes full circle touching lives.

About a year or so after John's shooting, I received a phone call from a woman who wanted to talk with me. She was someone I didn't know. She'd been given my name at our Christian bookstore in Ponca City, The Master's Touch. They'd often refer people to me when someone came into their store and would begin talking to them and asking if they could recommend a Christian woman that they could talk to.

I gave her directions to my home, and she arrived about a half hour later. She introduced herself and said that she appreciated me taking the time to visit with her and really needed to talk to someone to help her work out some problems in her life. I told her I loved helping people "get their ducks in a row," so to speak.

After visiting a few minutes, I asked her what she was struggling with and how I could help. She began, "Well, Mrs. Curl, before I get into why I came, I needed to share something with you."

"Okay. What do you need to tell me?"

"When they gave me your name at the bookstore, I just couldn't believe it. What I need to tell you first is I'm a nurse, and I used to work at the hospital here. I was on duty in the ER the night they brought your son in after he'd been shot."

"Oh my gosh. So you worked on John?"

"Yes, and Mrs. Curl, I don't mean to be graphic, but your son shouldn't be alive. He had brain matter coming out of his ears. He was the worst shooting victim I'd seen, but I've heard John's doing just fine now. Is that right?"

"Yes, he's doing great. He has to take medication to prevent seizures, but he's going on with his life, pretty healthy, thank God."

"Well, I just wanted to tell you some things that happened that night that really started me searching about God and stuff."

"Please, I want to hear about it."

"The doctors couldn't stabilize John's blood pressure," she continued. "It was all over the place, and it didn't look good for him to make it. He was very critical. You and your husband came into the ER room to see him, and it tore at my heart watching you as you touched him and cried for him. I thought for sure you were going to lose your son. About twenty minutes or so after you left the room, a man came in and asked if he could spend a few minutes with John. He told us he was your pastor. He stated his name, Pastor David Satterfield of First Assembly. We told him yes, he could see John.

"Mrs. Curl, you know those white curtains that hang from the ceiling on a bar in the ER area?"

"Yes," I said, "I think I know what you're talking about, the curtains you can pull all the way around to close off a patient for privacy?"

"Uh-huh, that's exactly right. The curtains were closed. I was standing where the curtains come together and could see into the area where John was. Your pastor laid both of his hands on John and started praying. The prayer was beautiful. Some of it I couldn't understand, but it was a powerful prayer. I say powerful because all of a sudden, while he was praying, those curtains just suddenly blew out, like somebody had opened a door to the outside and a strong wind came through. I mean, it was something to feel. I couldn't figure out what in the world was happening, but it made chills run up and down my arms. And somehow I knew it was something spiritual, even though I'm far from being a religious person. Then the pastor came out and thanked me for letting him see John. I went in to check John. His vitals had completely stabilized. That's when those of us attending to him knew he could be transferred to Tulsa on the medi-flight helicopter.

"I've never told anyone about what happened, until today. But it made me realize that I believe God must be real. I felt Him that night. I'd always wished I could have an opportunity to tell you about it, but I didn't know if I should. And then today when I was in the bookstore asking for a Christian woman to talk to, they gave me *your* name. Do you think that's a coincidence?"

"No," I said, "your being here is definitely *not* a coincidence. You're here because God had a divine appointment for us today."

We talked some more about how that encounter related to her life, and I thanked her for bringing her piece of the puzzle to what God had done in all our lives, even sharing all the wonderful things the Lord had done with John after he went to Tulsa for brain surgery. She was amazed. That's the only time I saw her, but I know as we sat in my home sharing, God took a snapshot of grace for me to store, share, and treasure.

Continuing in the next chapter, you'll read of how God tied up a lot of loose ends in His caring for us financially and so much more. May you be encouraged and feel God speaking to you through the retelling of this story. He's saying, *I love you.*

Whether you believe it or not, it doesn't change the fact that He does love you.

I'm discovering day by day the depth of His love. I'm not a Bible scholar. I have so much to learn, but of this one thing I am sure: God wants to show His love to us and to be intimately involved in our lives, to be a Father to us and help us live our lives, so we can be a beacon of His light to a very dark world.

Today, John is forty-five years old and married to Shirley, a precious woman whom we love like a daughter. He gave us Kortny, our granddaughter. He has a wonderful job and continues to live a whole and healthy life and is always ready to give an account of God's healing of his heart and his life, which he's told many times over the years, in large settings or one on one, as God continues to direct John's path for the Lord's glory and praise.

> There is an appointed time for everything, and there is a time for every event under heaven.
>
> Ecclesiastes 3:1

Paid in Full

> Understand, therefore that the Lord your God is the faithful God who for a thousand generations keeps His promises and constantly loves those who love Him and keeps His commands.
>
> Deuteronomy 7:9 (TLB)

Looming before us was a debt for John's medical bills, amounting to over $22,000 plus.

For a blue-collar family, that was huge. This was in 1982, and we lived from paycheck to paycheck like most middle class American families. My husband's insurance through his employer paid $15,000 of the $22,000, and for that we were thankful. However, the remaining $7,000, plus future expenses, was a daunting amount for us. We knew surgeries, medications, and doctors' bills lay in the future for John. We'd had many discussions about how we were going to manage to pay for these extra, unexpected expenses but all the while were so grateful that John was recovering wonderfully.

As you read in my story "On the Right Path," regarding the call on my life to go into a singing ministry, that ministry was just beginning when John's shooting occurred. As a result, I had put everything on hold. Attending to John was a main concern for me, and getting him back to his life was priority one. John was now well enough to go back to school, and normalcy was returning to our lives due to the grace of God.

I received a phone call from a church in northern Kansas, the pastor asking if I would be able to come to his church and give a morning and evening concert. He went on to say that he'd been told that I asked only for a love offering to be taken. I said, "That's right."

He continued, "Well, our church is very small, so I can't guarantee you'd even have your expenses met, but we'd really love for you to come if you could."

I told him that I didn't get hung up on numbers and that I'd love to accept the invitation. Once again he emphasized, "Well, I just don't want you to be disappointed at the size of the congregation. We're a small church, but we would still like you to come." I assured him that I would definitely be there.

"Just to make sure you understand, we are *really* small."

I was beginning to sense that he wanted me to ask, "How small?" So I did. "Okay, pastor, how small are we talking?"

"Ten in the morning and twelve in the evening. So will you still come?"

"Of course I will," I said, a little surprised but undaunted.

The drive was over three hours from my home to the northern Kansas church. I asked one of my friends to go with me. We left really early to arrive for their 10:30 a.m. service.

Unloading everything, Laveta and I set up my sound equipment, and then she went to sit in the congregation during the concert.

The pastor was so gracious and attentive, and no doubt you'd like to know, the number he gave was right on. There *were* ten people there.

I'll have to tell you the church building itself was a fairly large building, which surprised me. We found out later that day that the church congregation had split right after the new building was finished, due to the choice of the color of the carpeting. Christians certainly aren't perfect, just forgiven.

This poor pastor and his family had walked into the middle of a mess—a church that had split over a disagreement, and this was his first church to pastor.

As the concert progressed, God drew my attention to an older gentleman sitting by himself in the second pew, casually dressed in overalls. As I was singing, I kept looking at the old man. He had his arms crossed over his ample chest and belly, looking miserable. There was something about him that the Lord kept directing me to take notice of.

After the concert, I made a point of walking straight to him, extending my hand, and saying, "Hi, my name is Patty. I just wanted to thank you for coming this morning and to tell you that God loves you, and so do I."

With that said, as he pumped my hand, obviously embarrassed by what I'd told him, he spoke nervously, "Uh, well, I like your singing."

"Thank you. Will you be coming back tonight for the evening service?"

"No. I'm a busy farmer, and I don't come on Sunday evenings."

"I understand, but I hope you will change your mind. It would mean a lot to me if you came."

"Like I said, I've got lots to do, so I won't be coming." We parted. He went his way; I went mine.

The pastor and his wife had invited Laveta and me to have lunch with them and also offered us a place to rest in the afternoon before the evening concert. They had four little boys, cute kids, one wearing his hat to the side, locked and loaded, ready for anything, all of them looking like mischief waiting for a place to happen.

As we sat at their table and food was being brought, I couldn't help but notice that when the refrigerator was opened, all the food they seemed to have was being served to us. I began looking around the house, observing torn curtains and sparse furnishings. I realized that these precious people didn't have much, but what they had they were sharing with us. Their home was *very* clean and neat, but obviously they were struggling financially. I asked the pastor how they made ends meet with such a small congregation. He said that he supplemented his income by taking a part-time position as the janitor of a nursing home. *Wow,* I thought, *what a sacrifice of love.* Our conversation flowed easily, as I asked him if he could tell me something about the older man sitting in the second pew, the one in overalls.

"Oh, that's Ole Henry."

I told him that God had pointed him out to me that morning, but I didn't quite know what for. But I thought that the Lord wanted to do something in his life. I added that I had spoken to him after the concert, asking if he would be coming back that night. He told me no, saying he didn't come on Sunday nights. "Is that right?" I asked.

"That's true. I've never seen him on a Sunday night. Did the Lord show you anything in particular about Henry?"

"Actually, yes. I saw Henry behind a huge wall, like nothing could get past the wall he'd built to hide behind. Love couldn't get in or out, so Henry couldn't give or receive love. I could see this morning as God was pointing him out to me how miserable he was."

He smiled at me. "Let me say first, you sure picked a good one."

I smiled back, saying, "God picked him, not me." We both laughed.

"What the Lord showed you is right on, about the wall. Henry's wife died about two years ago, and he hasn't spoken to his children or grandchildren since then, all due to money. And he *is* miserable. He's an angry, miserable man, but he does come every Sunday morning."

"All we can do is pray that the Lord will bring him back tonight. And if indeed God wants to do something in Henry's life, He'll get him here." At that point, the pastor, his wife, Laveta, and I joined hands to pray for Henry and for the concert to touch lives.

After the meal, Laveta and I were shown to the boys' bedroom so we could rest. Looking at two bunk beds where the four little boys slept, we decided we'd each take a lower bunk.

I began to pray as I was lying in my bottom bunk, looking above my head and seeing mattress stuffing hanging from the upper bunk. That drew my thoughts back to the needs of the pastor's family. I started talking to Laveta lying in her bottom bunk across the room.

"You know, after praying, I believe the Lord would really want me to give whatever offering I receive to the pastor and his family."

"I get a witness to that, girlfriend."

"All right, then, motion carried." We broke out in joyful laughter. Neither of us actually slept, but the rest was nice, and we were ready for the evening, excited to see what the Lord had in store.

I was standing in the sanctuary getting my music tracks ready when Laveta came up behind me whispering, "Look, look, Patty, look who's here." There was such excitement in her voice. I turned around to look. Lo and behold, sitting there in the second pew in his overalls, arms crossed, looking just as miserable as he had that morning, was Ole Henry. Hallelujah! To say I was thrilled was an understatement. I knew it was going to be a wonderful evening.

I was introduced by the pastor. I walked out to the platform to greet the audience as they welcomed me with applause. I couldn't help myself; I had to count with my eyes to see if the twelve were there. There they were, exactly twelve, which included Henry, who wasn't supposed to be there, so somebody stayed home. I smiled to myself.

An offering was taken in the middle of the concert, as promised, and then I stepped back up to finish with a few more songs. As I was about to finish my last selection, God began to put into my thoughts to add a certain song, one I had not planned to do. In obedience, I told the audience that I had one more song, a last-minute addition. So I excused myself, laid down my microphone, and left the platform to get the tape from my briefcase.

As I was walking back, the Lord plainly urged me to sing that song *to* the old man in the second pew. Yes, to Henry. I was to sit in the first pew, turn around to face him, and sing directly to him as if no one else was in the room.

Okay, I thought.

So I went to the first pew, turned around, and began to sing. Henry was looking at me, gruff look on his face, arms still folded across his chest, looking miserable with eyes that seemed to be saying, "Go ahead, lady, you're not gonna move me; you're not gonna touch me."

The song was a Gaither song called "More of You." It talks about being empty and bare, having had your fill of things, yet still hungering and thirsting, then asking God to please hear your prayers for more, so much more of Him.

By the time I was about finished, Henry was leaning forward with his arms resting on the pew. His head was down on his arms, and he was weeping, loudly weeping. I saw the wall, coming down.

As I sang the last note, his head came up, tears streaming down his face. He got up and walked around to where I was. I laid my microphone down and stood up. Henry grabbed me, putting a bear hug on me. He hugged me so tightly bless his heart, that he almost broke every bone in my body. Then he said to me, "Girl, I love you. I truly do." He was smiling and crying at the same time.

"I love you too, Henry."

Taking me by the shoulders, he said, "Do you know how long it's been since I said those three words?" He paused, trying to get the words out. "It's been a very, long, time, and I tell you what, I can't wait to get home to call my kids and my grandkids to tell them I love them."

"Henry, that is wonderful. But I want to tell you how personal God is, how much He loves you. He pointed you out to me this morning. He has seen the tears on your pillow at night. He's heard your cry to be set free from your wall, so He brought a little Oklahoma gal from three hours away to sing to you. He brought you back on a Sunday night, the night you don't usually come to church, to give you that gift, to break down that wall." Henry smiled at me.

The tears started flowing again as he said, "He did that for me."

"He sure did. This was *all* God's doing. That's how well He knows all of us."

He thanked me as he was walking away. I couldn't help but notice the change in his countenance. He was strolling down the aisle like he didn't have a care in the world, and he didn't.

There was intermittent applause as others sitting near Henry could see the healing of his heart taking place. Many had prayed, I'm sure, for Henry to be free of his unforgiveness of his family. All who knew Henry's story were so touched by what had happened to him. Everyone was very grateful that God had arranged a snapshot of grace, a true divine appointment for Henry.

After everyone left, Laveta and I were packing up my equipment to start for home. The pastor approached me, saying how thankful he was that God had brought me to his church. Several had accepted Christ in the morning service, and he was rejoicing for that. We all rejoiced over Henry's healed heart as well. He then handed me a check, which was the love offering. I took the check and saw the amount of $60, which, in my opinion, was a lot for that small congregation. I turned it over, endorsed it, and handed it back to the pastor. Confused, he said, "Is there something wrong with the check?"

"No, I just wanted you to have it."

"What? I can't take this. You gave two glorious concerts, touched lives, ministered to all of us. You need gas to drive three hours home, and you'll need to buy supper. I can't take this."

"Pastor, if you're going to argue with somebody, you'll have to argue with God, because He's the one who put the idea in my heart."

He got big tears in his eyes as he said, "You don't know what this means to my family, thank you."

"I think I do," I said. "Your love for the Lord and your willingness to serve Him in all circumstances hasn't gone unnoticed. God noticed, and so did I. You and your wife shared your home, your food, and your love with Laveta and me. I can't thank you enough for inviting me to come." There were parting hugs all around. He then helped us load the car, and we took off for home.

Our hearts were so full we were flying, awestruck by what God had done.

Unbeknownst to me, God wasn't finished yet.

Approaching the last gas station on our way out of town, I pulled in. "Gotta get gas," I said.

Laveta grabbed my arm before I got out of the car and said, "You remember today when we were resting on our bunks, you said the Lord had put it on your heart to give your offering to the pastor and his family?"

"Yeah, I remember."

Speaking with a laugh, she said, "Well, you know what? He told me I was to fill your gas tank, so there!"

"Laveta, I can't let you do that."

Speaking with determination, she said, "Well, if you're gonna argue with somebody, you'll have to argue with God, because He put me up to it."

That sounded vaguely familiar, enough said. "Thank you, my friend, and thank you, Lord."

Back on the road, we'd been driving about an hour. It was about 9:30 p.m., and we were both hungry. The noon lunch was no more than a memory to our stomachs. I saw a small café up the road and pulled in.

It was a cute place and very clean, a Mom and Pop restaurant containing about ten tables. The food was fabulous, just great home cooking. Enjoying the meal more than I had in restaurants in a long time, I decided to thank the person who cooked it. Grabbing a napkin, pen in hand, I wrote "Dear Cook, I've traveled through a lot of states, eaten at many restaurants, but I haven't tasted anything that compares with your food. Just wanted you to know how much you're appreciated. Also wanted to tell you, God loves you." I signed it Patty Curl, from Oklahoma. I motioned for the waitress and gave her the napkin, asking her to please give it to the cook. After leaving a tip, we headed to the cashier with our tickets in hand.

Someone hollered, "Which one is she?" I turned around to see what was going on. There was a very stout man, wearing a once white apron like a badge of honor displaying all his cooking prowess. He was waving my napkin.

The waitress pointed at me, saying, "That's her, the blonde one."

He walked up to me and grabbed my ticket and Laveta's, saying, "You're not paying for your food. No one has taken the time to tell me how much they appreciated my food. And no one's *ever* told me that God loves me." He tore up our tickets. "Thank you. You can eat here any time." He gave me a hug and went back to his kitchen.

Okay, think on this. Checklist of needs: Gas, *check.* Food, *check.* Was God done? Not by a long shot.

We arrived in Ponca City about 12:30 a.m. I dropped Laveta at her house. Her husband was waiting for her. I thanked him for letting her go with me. I arrived home about 12:45 a.m., took my shower, and was in bed by 1:30 a.m. Spencer was glad that I was safely home.

The phone rang at 7:30 a.m. I sleepily grabbed it. "Hello?" It was a man's voice. "Is this Mrs. Curl? Is John Curl your son?"

"Yes to both."

"Well, Mrs. Curl, my name is Joe Wideman, District Attorney of Kay County."

With that little piece of information, I was wide awake. My heart began pounding wildly. *Why is he calling? Is something wrong?* "Uh, yes, sir, what can I do for you?"

"Your son was the victim of a shooting recently, is that right?"

"Yes."

"So how is John doing?"

"Much better, thank you. We take it one day at a time helping him deal with what happened, but we're thankful for how far he's come. He is facing another surgery but thankful to be alive."

"Glad to hear that. Mrs. Curl, have you ever heard of the Victim Assistance Program?"

"No."

"Well, we help victims of a crime, like your son."

"What does that entail?"

"We pay for everything that your insurance doesn't pay for. That includes all future surgeries and all medications needed due to this injury for John's lifetime."

I had no breath. "What? You pay for what?"

Before another word was spoken, at that very moment, God spoke this to me, *Patty, for your gift of $60 to that pastor, I give you $7,000 plus to pay the debt.*

As I was writing this, I experienced the same breathless moment of being wondrously overwhelmed by my heavenly Father.

"Thank you so much, Mr. Wideman."

"You're welcome, Mrs. Curl. Someone from the Victim Assistance Program will be in touch with you. You will be assigned an advocate who will help you file the necessary papers to apply for the money. Good luck to you and John."

I was speechless and stunned, dropping to my knees to give thanks to the giver of every good gift—my Lord.

A burden lifted!

A week or so later, a woman called from Victims Assistance. Judy and I worked together diligently to get all of the paperwork ready. She would be presenting John's case to a committee in Oklahoma City for approval of the funds. Judy had told us it was more or less a done deal and that we'd be approved. It was just a matter of formality with nothing to worry about. I talked with her before she left to drive to Oklahoma City. She assured me she would call me with the good news as soon as she arrived home.

Enter the *enemy,* "the one who seeks to steal, to kill and destroy" (John 10:10).

The phone rang. It was Judy. "Patty, I don't know how to tell you this, but they denied the funds. I don't understand what happened. I'm totally confused."

"What in the world happened? Why did they deny his case? Did they give a reason?"

"I'm as surprised about this as you are, and they gave no reason. They just said, 'Denied.'"

I was thinking at that moment, *Okay, Lord, I know you gave this to us. What do we need to do here?*

"All right, Judy. What recourse do we have?"

"We can appeal."

"Let's do it. What do we need to do?"

She told me she would get all of the paperwork prepared again, file the appeal, and we would get a new hearing.

I said, "Judy, this time I want to go with you."

Weeks passed before we were given a new hearing on our appeal.

The day came. She and I drove to Oklahoma City to some state offices. The hearing was in a large conference room with a huge table in the middle where the committee would sit. Chairs were placed against the walls around the room for those of us who had hearings that day. It was a daunting, confidence-busting atmosphere.

We all settled into our seats around 9:00 a.m. The committee walked into the room and took their seats around the table. At the head of the table a very striking and attractive African American woman took the seat of authority. She introduced herself as the chairwoman. I'm not an expert at guessing age, but she looked to be in her fifties and exuded confidence and control.

She brought the hearings to order, stating that she would read the list of cases to be heard that day in the order they'd be heard. We were listening for the name John Curl. The list was very long, maybe thirty to forty names. Ours was the very last name on the list, the last one read. I whispered to Judy, "I guess we can leave and come back in a couple of hours, huh?"

She leaned over. "No, we have to stay here the whole day. You never know how fast things will move, and if you're not here when they call your name, you don't get your hearing."

Oh boy, I thought.

My thoughts were suddenly interrupted. The chairwoman was speaking. "Now that I have read the list, I have something to say. Is there anyone in the room representing John Curl, the last name on the list?" Judy raised her hand, and I slowly raised mine, unsure if I was even supposed to.

"Who are you?" she asked Judy. Judy told her that she was our Victim Assistance representative. The chairwoman then pointed to me, since I had raised my hand, and asked, "And what is your name?"

Standing up, I said, "I'm Patty Curl, John Curl's mother."

She looked at me and said, "You're the one I want to talk to."

Judy looked at me with a double-take, like "What?" I was thinking the same thing. *Lady, how did you even know I'd be here? I just came along for the ride.*

A reminder to me that my Lord was chairing the meeting.

The chairwoman thanked me and asked me to sit back down.

The room was packed to the hilt, I wasn't even supposed to be there, and now I was the center of attention.

She began, "The Lord woke me in the middle of the night."

Okay, wait a minute, I thought. My antenna went up. *Christian sister in the room, a believer, she just said the Lord woke her up. All right, Lord, I know you're here, thank you.*

She continued, "He woke me up to tell me we had not done right by John Curl. So, Mrs. Curl, I owe you an apology from me personally and for the committee. So we will be moving John Curl's case from last on the list to the top of the list. We'll be hearing his case first."

I looked over at Judy, who was looking shocked and a little green. Needless to say, I was stunned at this turn of events, but God was in the room, big time! Judy raised her hand, asking if we could have a few minutes to prepare.

The chairwoman called for a ten-minute recess.

We stepped out of the room. Judy laid her paper-laden briefcase on a bench and said to me, "Patty, I have got to go into the bathroom."

"Okay, but hurry though."

She disappeared into the bathroom.

Minutes passed, more minutes passed. A woman came out of the conference room and said, "Mrs. Curl, ten minutes are up. We're ready for you. Where is your representative?"

"In the bathroom."

"Go get her."

I went into the bathroom and heard the sounds of someone throwing up. *Oh no,* I thought. "Judy, is that you?"

"Yes. I'm so sick. Patty, you're going to have to present the case."

"Do what?"

"You'll be fine. Take my briefcase. All of the papers are in there."

I walked out of the bathroom in a daze.

"All right, Lord, You've brought me here for a reason," I prayed. "You tell me in Psalm 139 that You go before me and encompass me from behind, so I'm going to stand on Your word that You've prepared the way before me, and You'll give me the words to say, the courage to do it, and results are *Yours,* not man's. So I know I'm in the best place possible, the center of Your will, so thank You, Lord, and I love You."

I walked into the conference room and explained to the committee about Judy being sick and unable to speak to them. "So if you'll allow me to do so, I'll speak for my son's case."

The chairwoman said, "Absolutely, Mrs. Curl. Proceed."

So it began.

I basically gave them John's testimony of that day. All of the gathering of information I'd done out of my wanting to know what happened really paid off.

Then, because I knew I had a Christian sister in a place of power in the room, I began to tell of every miraculous detail, as I shared with you, the reader, in "Our Isaac."

I'm telling you, you could have heard a pin drop. There wasn't a dry eye in the room. When God moves, I mean, He moves!

"Mrs. Curl," she began, "your appeal is approved. You were eloquent, precise, informative, and a pleasure to listen to. I can say for myself, I was truly blessed." They applauded me, wow.

I thanked them and then said, "I do have one question, if I may?"

"Certainly, what is it?"

"Well, I was just wondering why you denied John's case the first time."

"Mrs. Curl, you have every right to know that. We assumed that your son and some other boys were out at the lake drinking and horsing around, with a gun in the mix. So our assumption was that it was a party gone badly, and John was injured. After hearing your testimony today and also finding out that John didn't even know the man who committed the crime, that John was there frog-gigging, and most importantly, that you had asked the doctors to take a blood sample that night to see if there was alcohol in John's system because you wanted to know. And as we heard today, your documents proved that John had no traceable alcohol in his body; our assumptions were totally wrong.

"Mrs. Curl, I know now that is why the Lord woke me and told me we had not done right by your son. Again, we apologize for going on an assumption."

"God made it right, didn't He?" I said, smiling at her. She nodded and returned the smile.

Our financial need: $7,000, *check.* Future costs for John's lifetime, *check.*

An account of the multiple blessings of God are in order here, starting with my trip to sing at the Kansas church.

First, the divine appointment with Henry, changing his life and as a ripple effect the lives of Henry's family and the church family who witnessed it.

Also, meeting a financial need of the pastor and God blessing the pastor's love for his congregation and his service to Him.

Allowing Laveta to be a part of the blessings as she paid for the fuel during the trip to Kansas.

God touching the heart of the cook in the restaurant who had never been told that God loved him and the additional blessing of our food being paid for.

The blessing of the Victim's Assistance call from the district attorney.

God orchestrating the appeal, using a daughter of His to chair the meeting at the Victim's Assistance hearing. A Christian woman who listened to His still, small voice in the middle of the night and had the courage to acknowledge God in an open forum.

The blessing of giving me the opportunity to share God's healing of our son in every detail so God could receive the glory.

And lastly, God bringing forth the truth, righting a wrong. And for all the lives touched over the years by the telling of this story.

All glory and honor belong to Him. *I love You with all of my heart, Lord.*

> What's more, I am with you, and will protect you wherever you go, and will bring you back safely to this land; I will be with you constantly until I have finished giving you all I am promising.
>
> Genesis 28:15 (TLB)

The Story of the Sheep

Know that the Lord is God. It is He who made us, and we are His people, the sheep of His pasture.

Psalm 100:3 (NIV)

Sometimes, among daily life experiences, we can find the greatest life lessons if we listen closely and see with eyes of expectation. Snapshots of grace will unfold before us, gifts to be tucked away in our hearts to be remembered, treasured, and shared. So I share with you "The Story of the Sheep," one of the most moving examples of intercession I have ever witnessed.

Our home is in a rural area. On the north side of our house, there's a pasture where cattle graze lazily. The west side of the house faces our neighbor's pasture, where they raise sheep.

Over the years, I've been fascinated by these animals. I can view them from my kitchen window while I wash dishes and peer through the curtains, watching as the sheep interact with one another. In fact, many times I've gone out on my back porch, contentedly sitting and observing them for hours. I've learned a great deal from watching, such as when the sheep graze, they always seem to be aware of where one another are, constantly looking up from grazing to view the rest of the flock.

One of the things that sparked my interest was when the ewes gave birth I could see a natural maternal instinct, as expected. But if there were a threat from an intruder, like a pack of dogs, the adult sheep (both male and female) would circle the young lambs in the center and would stand facing out, daring the intruders to touch their young, a caring display of affection I hadn't expected.

But the most endearing and even touching scene I watched unfold one afternoon will not soon be forgotten by yours truly. I thought the only thing sheep cared about was being fed, watered, and having plenty of grass to eat; however, a gift was awaiting my attention, something God wanted me to learn, a discovery to deepen my view of Him and His hand on His creation.

The lambs were several months old now, exploring their surroundings. I was busily getting my kitchen cleaned, which included washing my dishes. As was my custom to make the job go faster, I began to look through my kitchen curtains to see what the sheep might be up to. As I looked, I saw a lone lamb that seemed to be struggling, moving its head back and forth, but couldn't change his position. I continued to watch with concern as the movements would escalate then stop. It seemed the lamb had grown tired of the struggle. Not only did my concerns begin to grow but also my curiosity.

I couldn't quite see well enough from the window to know what was truly going on, so I stopped what I was doing and decided to go out on my back porch to get a better look. Stepping outside, I now had a better vantage point and could see that this young lamb had managed to get its head caught in the fence at the bottom of the pasture. It was struggling with all the strength it could muster to free itself to no avail. Exhaustion had set in. Its bleating reflected the fact that it must have been caught in the snare for a while. I decided to climb the barbed wire fence that separated our yard from the pasture to see if I could help the lamb free itself. As I was approaching the fence, I just had a sense that I was not to intervene, but just stand, watch, and learn.

As I was trying to process those thoughts, I began to wonder where the rest of the sheep were. They were nowhere in sight, and usually the flock were in close proximity to one another. While that question was passing through my mind, I heard the sound of many sheep bleating, almost in unison. I admit I'd never heard them raising their voices so simultaneously before, and with such alarm and urgency.

I leaned down to get a better look under the limbs of trees that blocked a clearer view. My eyes began to follow the sound my ears were hearing. There, at the top of the hill, on the other side of the pasture, by the fence next to the farmer's house, stood the whole flock.

They were all facing the house and bleating as loudly as they could. It seemed as if they were sounding an alarm. They wanted to be heard. The door of the house opened, and the farmer stepped out and opened the gate to the pasture. As soon as the sheep saw him, they began to turn and run to the lone lamb that was caught in the fence. It looked for all the world that they were saying, "One of our own is in trouble, so we're pleading for him."

The farmer followed the flock to the bottom of the pasture, and seeing the lamb caught in the fence, he hurriedly walked up to the animal, grabbed its head, and began trying to work it free. The rest of the flock stood motionless, watching, waiting.

Finally, the lamb was free.

The once tired and exhausted lamb, now experiencing its new freedom, began to kick up its hooves as if rejoicing, bounding this way and that. The other sheep then began to get caught up in the celebration and started jumping, kicking, and turning. It was a sight to see.

I stood watching this whole scene with tears in my eyes yet a smile across my lips, as I realized what God was trying to show me through His creation, what a beautiful picture of intercession I had just watched unfold, a true snapshot He wanted me to treasure. I'm thankful to God for making that moment, a divine appointment.

We all get caught in the snares of life, struggling to free ourselves, and get too tired to try anymore.

Sometimes prayer won't even come because of our tiredness and discouragement; then God begins to speak to hearts to pray.

Just as the flock stood outside the master's house, those in prayer stand and plead for us.

The master hears; He comes and sets us free. We *rejoice* together!

I thought to myself, *No wonder the Lord calls us His sheep,* remembering the verse:

> If a man has a hundred sheep, and one wanders away and is lost, what will he do? Won't he leave the ninety and nine others and go out into the hills to search for the lost one, and when he finds it, he will rejoice over it, more than the ninety and nine who are safe.
>
> Matthew 18:12 (TLB)

Life has taught me that we all take turns in the snares of life. People pass by us every day, struggling with hopelessness, not knowing where to turn, and with thoughts of giving up. This sheep story has taught me to try to always have my ear and my spirit attuned to the still, small voice of the Shepherd, as He wants to speak someone's name to us so we can be the intercessors, standing in the gap for those who cannot pray for themselves. Just as Christ is our intercessor, pleading on our behalf, we need to be intercessors for those who have been ensnared in life situations. As the definition of intercessor says: "one who pleads on behalf of another."

My companions were hopelessness, fear, discouragement, and exhaustion for days as I struggled to pray for my son as he fought for his life. He had been the victim of an accidental shooting; a bullet lodged in his brain. All hope seemed lost. The doctors told us that his chances-for survival were slim at best, and *if* he lived, he would be a vegetable. A young man who just turned seventeen with all of his life before him was standing at the door of death. After many days at the hospital and sitting by the bedside of my son, recovering from brain surgery, still not knowing the final outcome of his future, prayers wouldn't come. I was struggling just to keep it together, to be strong. My faith was intact, as well as my trust for my Lord, but I couldn't seem to pray anymore. Sheer exhaustion had taken over. In the darkness of the hospital room, God spoke to my heart, *Rest, my daughter. I am speaking John's name to others to pray.* He then reminded me of the sheep and that He knew of us being caught in a snare, and He was with us. Peace, sweet peace, flooded my soul.

I hope you will always carry the sheep story close to your heart.

The Broken Chair

> Create in me a clean heart O Lord, and renew a steadfast spirit within me.
>
> Psalm 51:10

Working with youth has always been a passion of mine. Helping them recognize their value was my chosen topic when speaking at schools and community events. As a speaker for over twenty-five years for adult groups as well, I discovered that people of all ages and walks of life need to hear of their value. The world tells us something totally different if we don't look a certain way or have certain material things. That is not at all where our value lies.

As we all sometimes do, we see the value in others while not always recognizing it in those closest to us. I too found myself to be guilty of that very thing concerning my son who, as a teenager, made some very bad choices that were alcohol related and that had tremendous negative consequences on his life and ours as well. Brushes with the law, car accidents, and injuries sustained as a result of wrong behavior nearly took his life several times, as you read in "Our Isaac" about him being accidentally shot while being in the wrong place at the wrong time. All these consequences, strongly limited his choices for a future. I didn't realize how much I had devalued my son because of his devastating choices, ironically while I was telling others about their value.

I never stopped loving him or harbored any unforgiveness, but God knew this mother's heart needed changing, for indeed I had wrong thinking and wrong attitudes toward John.

God chose a wonderful way to make things right.

John was facing DUI charges, and was sentenced in the month of December to eighteen months in prison. He was to begin serving his sentence in January. He had lost everything—home, job, and finances. Having nothing, he asked to come home for the month of December.

During that month, healing of hearts was taking place. God was at work. We were laughing with each other, which was very special. Hurts and disappointments had overshadowed any laughter over the last few years.

Christmas was soon approaching. John told me that he wanted to give me a gift; however, having no money to purchase a gift, he said, "Mom, I found something on one of my nature walks, and I want to fix it up and give it to you for Christmas, but I need for you to drive me back to where I used to live." I told him he didn't need to give me anything. Just having him at home was enough of a gift.

Per John's request, I drove him to the town where he had lived. He directed me to a wooded area where he took long walks alone. Getting out of the car, he asked me to remain there until he returned. About twenty-five minutes later, he came back carrying what I would describe as the biggest mess of broken wood I had ever seen.

I got out of the car to look at what he was holding. There were many broken pieces that had obviously been under water, for the wood was soaked, covered with slime and algae, and stunk terribly, and he wanted to put the mess in the trunk of my car. I again looked at it and said, "Son, what in the world is this?"

"It's what is left of a chair, Mom. I want to fix it up for you for Christmas."

Looking at the broken pieces, I said, "John, I don't hold out much hope for that chair. Someone obviously threw it away because it was irreparably damaged; it couldn't be fixed."

We were standing there looking at each other when John squared his shoulders and said, "Mom, you're just gonna have to trust me, 'cause when I get done with it, it's gonna be beautiful." Relenting, I opened the trunk.

As the holidays drew closer, John worked secretly on his gift in his dad's workshop, not allowing us to view his work. He went about sanding and polishing, nailing and gluing.

Christmas morning came. After breakfast, John went outside to get his treasure. I, on the other hand, wasn't expecting much. He walked in carrying an absolutely gorgeous chair. It was a Queen Anne style chair, made of solid cherry wood, a deeply warm and beautiful color. The curves on the top part of the chair glistened after all the loving care John had given it, restored to near perfection. I was looking at something totally unexpected.

I stood there smiling and crying at the same time with my jaw on the floor. He grinned at me. "Mom, do you like it?"

"Oh, honey, not only do I like it, but I never thought in a million years that something so broken and ugly could become that beautiful."

As I said those words, the Lord brought to my heart the thoughts that I'd been looking at John's life just as I had looked at that broken chair. I thought that he too was irreparably damaged, beyond repair, no longer able to be fixed. God reminded me that He was in the restoration business. At that moment, God repeated to my heart the words John had spoken that day standing at the trunk of the car: *You're just going to have to trust Me, because when I get through with your son, he's going to be beautiful. He needs a lot of repairing and restoring, and just as John sanded and polished that chair, I will sand and polish your son.*

As the Lord gently changed my heart, tears of joy ran down my cheeks. John and I hugged for a long moment, and I said to him, "Please forgive me for ever devaluing you, for looking at what you'd done, not who you are, someone whom God loves and values enough that He gave his Son for you and is giving you another chance to be all you can be. I love you so much, John."

I call the chair "John's chair." It has a special place in my dining room. No one is allowed to sit on it. I was given an old piece of needlepoint tapestry while on a speaking trip to Illinois. The couple whose home I stayed in restored old Victorian homes, and she had found this tapestry in an old trunk in an attic. I had shared with her about John's chair, and she thought this tapestry would be perfect to cover the seat of the chair. And it was a perfect fit. So it's in pristine condition now. But the beauty of the chair was only enhanced by the tapestry. The beauty was there all along in my son's eyes. Beauty *is* in the eye of the beholder. I only have to look at it to remember how far John has come, for he's becoming that beautiful young man God promised. It's taken him many years to straighten his life out, but he's accomplishing that day by day.

You see, when John found that chair, broken, lying in water, covered in slime, he wasn't seeing any of that; he was seeing with his heart the finished product. That's the way our heavenly Father sees us, what we can be when we give Him the broken pieces of our lives.

> Now your attitudes and thoughts must all be constantly changing for the better. Yes, you must be a new and different person, holy and good. Clothe yourself with this new nature.
>
> Ephesians 4:23, 24 (TLB)

I've seen, as I've shared John's broken chair to many audiences over the years, people responding by asking for prayer to give their brokenness back to the Lord for Him to restore, to erase their mistakes, and to give them a brand-new start. Parents have approached me who have, like me, devalued their children because of their actions and wives who had devalued their husbands. All had suddenly recognized that their hearts and attitudes needed changing.

One of the best responses to sharing that story was a young woman and her mother who came to talk with me following the meeting where I'd spoken. The girl began telling me her story, with tears streaming off of her chin, saying she was the broken chair. She'd been a drug addict for several years and had been, as she put it, "to hell and back," taking her parents with her. She continued, "I didn't know until today that I could be restored and given a chance to start over with a clean slate. But today I prayed the prayer with you to accept Jesus as my Savior, and I now know... I really know *I am changed.*" Her mom hugged me and said, "We've prayed and waited for many years for this to happen. God has given our daughter back to us."

God is the *builder* and *restorer* of lives.

64 Cents

I related "The Broken Chair" to you in the previous chapter regarding my and my son's restored relationship, but I'd like to tell you more about the month that our son stayed with us prior to beginning his prison term of eighteen months as a result of DUI charges.

We were dreading that day but were determined to make the time John was with us special, making up for lost time, reaching back to remember the times when we laughed, teased, and cut up with each other.

The day was drawing closer that I would have to give up my son to the prison system to begin serving his one-and-a-half-year sentence for his offenses, a very hard thing to do. We did not speak of what was to come. We tried to live in the moment, savoring every minute we had together. The time for blame was over; now was about enjoying one another again.

The day arrived.

Walking out to the car, we were both quiet. Even as I write, emotions rise up within me as I vividly remember those moments.

We were trying to keep a stiff upper lip, each for the sake of the other. As we sat in the car, John said, "Mom, hold out your hand." I did as he asked. He placed several coins in the palm of my hand and slowly closed my fingers around them, saying, "This is all I have left, Mom. It's 64 cents. Keep it for me, will you?"

There was a serious pause as I was deciding whether to cry or try to lighten the all too painful reality of the moment. But God had arranged for a snapshot of grace in the form of laughter and relief through a few small coins, just 64 cents. A small thing to be sure, but a huge impact on our spirit. A light moment, much needed, to help us through the weight of the day.

"So, honey, did you want me to invest this for you?" We burst out laughing at the same time.

"Yeah, Mom, that would be great. How much interest do you think it'll make in eighteen months?" We laughed again, heartier this time, alleviating the stress we were both feeling.

This was getting harder, then and now.

We arrived at the courthouse, parked, and began the walk that would change our lives.

What do you do? What do you say? My precious son was going to be totally out of my care, my heart was gripped by fear beyond anything I can describe, but God was preparing a divine appointment for us.

The large, open waiting area in the courthouse was full of people, those who were there to receive final sentencing and family who had come to support them in spite of the mistakes committed. That's what families do.

The room consisted of nothing but concrete and marble. It was cold, uninviting, and sobering, with voices echoing off of the cold walls.

Why am I in this place? How did we get here? Where did we take a very wrong turn? All of these questions flooded my mind. Then came the big question that I was trying to keep from voicing, but it rose up in my spirit: *Lord, where are You in all of this? I need You.*

Still waiting for John's name to be called, my thoughts took off to a safer place.

I started remembering when John was twelve years old. He had come into our bedroom during the night and, waking me, said, "Mama, I want to have Christ as my Savior." That woke me up for sure. I took him out of the bedroom so we would not wake his dad. He began telling me that he wanted to have Jesus in his heart. He said, "I know He's real, Mom, 'cause I've seen Him in you, Bamma, Bampa, and Debbie (his grandparents and my sister)." I explained to him what he needed to believe in his heart about Christ, to believe that Jesus is God's only Son, sent from heaven to become a man to live among us and to die on a cross, taking away our sin. After dying, Jesus was buried and three days later rose again to show that He conquered death for us, and because He lives in heaven with his Father now, we can live there too, when God calls us to come home. But Jesus will live in our hearts now if we ask Him to.

I asked John if he believed that, and he said, "Yes, Mama, I do." So I held him close, and we prayed the salvation prayer together. It was a wonderful moment.

That is not an adequate description. It was an awesome, glorious moment! Not only did my son accept Christ, settling his eternity, but God in His goodness had let me be the one who prayed with him. A few nights later, my daughter, Lori, who was almost fourteen, woke me and asked me to pray the prayer with her. I was overwhelmed with thanks to God for bringing my children into a personal relationship with Him through believing in Christ. It was another heart-warming privilege as I held my daughter and prayed with her.

Jolted back to the present by someone saying my name, I looked up. Standing there in that cold, sobering courthouse was a man from my church. He was wearing a uniform. I said, "Hi, J.B. What are you doing here?"

"I work here. I'm a bailiff."

"You are? I had no idea you worked here."

"Sure do. I saw John's name on the docket for today, so I thought you might need someone to pray for you."

Wow! Okay, let's pause here for a minute. Let's take an inventory of the needs and the meeting of those needs once again to count our blessings:

I needed an answer to my question, *Lord, where are You in all of this? I need You.*

I needed peace in this horrible, confusing time. The answer: He took my thoughts to remembering John's salvation prayer, every sweet detail of it, and that remembrance brought peace to my mind. John belonged to God; both John and Lori belonged to Him.

More blessing inventory: I needed to know that God knew where we were and what we were facing. The answer: He sent J.B., the court bailiff (a man from my church), to find me and to ask if he could pray for us.

If that isn't evidence of a true heavenly Father showing His love, I don't know what is.

J.B. sat down on the concrete bench between John and me, laying one hand on each of us, and began to pray.

Voices were again echoing off of those cold, marble walls, reverberating to everyone within hearing distance. Some lowered their voices but continued to talk; most bowed their heads in respect to the prayer being raised. What an incredible happening—*God cares.*

John's name was called along with several others. He and I walked into the courtroom to await our turn. I noticed that most of those called along with John were being sentenced for DUI offenses as well. They were systematically handcuffed, shackled at the ankles, and led out of the courtroom.

The peace from the prayer lingered with me, but my mother's heart was breaking at the thought of John being handcuffed and shackled. I whispered a silent prayer, *Lord, I don't think I can handle seeing John shackled.* I didn't request that God change the circumstances; I only said that I couldn't bear to watch.

John's turn came. He stepped before the judge, and his charges were read. The judge asked, "How do you plead?"

John said, "Guilty, sir." No argument, denial, or excuses, being a man by taking responsibility for his actions.

For that, I was proud of him.

With the sentence pronounced, deputies stepped forward with handcuffs and shackles. John held out his hands. The judge looked up from his bench and said, "No restraints are necessary, son. Walk on over to the jail with the deputies. They will get you processed."

My heart leapt into my throat. I wanted to stand up and yell, "Thank you!"

God had reached into that courtroom, touched that judge, and soothed a mama's heart, in one fell swoop. Why? Because He loves us, all of us.

A railing separated me from John. The deputy allowed John to lean across to tell me good-bye. I reached out, grabbed my boy and held on tight, I didn't want to let go. I knew I had to release him, not just from the embrace, but into God's care, for I had gone as far as *I* could go.

"I love you, Mom," John said.

"I love you too, John. Take care of yourself honey. Remember we love you. I'll come see you as soon as I'm allowed to visit." I held back tears; I knew it would upset him to see me crying.

"Mom," he said as he was walking away, "I'm sorry. Tell Dad I'm sorry, okay?"

"I will, honey. Just remember that we love you no matter what. I'll pray for you every day."

"Thanks Mom," he said, with one last, "I love you," as he walked out of the courtroom.

Driving home was *so* hard. Even though John was no longer with me in the car, the smell of his aftershave lingered there. It gave me comfort but at the same time broke my heart. He was *really* gone, to a place I couldn't begin to imagine.

The trip home seemed endless. As I pulled into our driveway, I just sat there completely exhausted and empty. Resting my arms and head on the steering wheel, I whispered, "God, please take care of him. I know he put himself in this place, but I ask You to be merciful. You have kept him through so many dangers, and I thank You, Lord."

I stepped out of my car onto our sand and gravel driveway. Looking down, I saw John's footprints in the sand and lost it. I didn't know when I would see him again. Through my tears, I started walking inside, willing my legs to move. Once inside, I really let go. The dam burst with everything I'd been holding back, the brokenness I was feeling, the uncertainty of it all, yet knowing all the while God was supplying my needs.

I decided to call my brother, Jimmy, in Virginia. I needed to talk things through. I shared all that had transpired that day, the hard things as well as the wonderful ways God had provided for us.

As Jimmy listened, he knew I needed reassurance. He began, "Sis, you talked about seeing John's footprints in the sand. Do you remember the poem about footprints?"

"Yes, some of it."

"Well, just like in the poem, there had been two sets of footprints in the sand as Jesus was walking alongside; then there was only one set of footprints, and Jesus said, 'That is when I picked you up and carried you. The footprints are Mine.'"

That was just what I needed to hear—God's assurance flooded my soul. Those *are* Christ's footprints; He is carrying us. His love reached all the way to where I was, and His love followed John to wherever this difficult journey took him.

> When you go through deep waters and great trouble, I will be with you. When you go through rivers of great difficulty, you will not drown. When you walk through the fire of oppression, you will not be burned up. The flames will not consume you. For I am the Lord your God, your Savior, the Holy One of Israel.
>
> Isaiah 43: 2–3 (TLB)

> Though I am surrounded by troubles You will bring me safely through them. You will clench Your fist against my angry enemies. Your power will save me. The Lord will work out His plans for my life, for Your loving kindness Lord, continues forever.
>
> Psalm 138: 7–8 (TLB)

The Foot Washing

> All these blessings will come upon you and accompany you if you obey the Lord your God.
>
> Deuteronomy 28:2 (NIV)

I think we're all a little guilty of keeping score of wrongs committed against us.

Being a woman, I think women have more of a tendency to be scorekeepers of wrongs. When we get into arguments, we tend to pull out all of the little things and sometimes big things from years back, most forgotten by the men but certainly not forgotten by us ladies. As my dad has said many times, "Women are like elephants. They never forget anything." I think there's truth to that statement. I lived it. I had no idea that I was keeping a scorecard of hurts, disappointments, and failings on my husband, a card that was affecting our relationship and our marriage. After fifteen years of marriage, I'd decided that

I was so unhappy I wanted it to end. My husband was totally unaware of these feelings.

While standing in church one Sunday morning, the Lord spoke to my heart, *Patty, you don't even pray for Spencer anymore.* That hit me like a ton of bricks. I hadn't prayed for my husband, in a long time. I remember telling God, "Lord, if You want me to stay in this marriage, You're going to have to give me respect for him and love for him, because right now I have neither."

As I stood in the congregation, I heard the pastor asking for people to come forward if they had a need, and he'd pray for us. I felt a nudge. *Go forward, and I will take care of the rest.* I walked to the front as the pastor moved from person to person; then he stood in front of me asking me the need I wanted him to pray for. I told him to just pray for me however he wanted, which he did. Then he said, "Patty, why don't you spend a little time here at the altar, just you and God." I knelt down.

A close friend of mine was playing the organ. When the service ended, I was still at the altar, and Carol was still playing music. It was just her, me, and God in the sanctuary. I can tell you that while I knelt there it was as though God was pouring a pitcher of liquid love down over my head. When I got up from the altar, all of the anger was gone, and hope had taken its place.

A few days later, during my quiet time with the Lord and while reading Scripture, I read about Jesus washing the disciples' feet. "Then, He (Jesus) poured water into the basin and began to wash the disciples' feet" (John 13:5). As I was thinking about that, the Lord placed the thought in my mind, *I want you to wash Spencer's feet.*

You might be asking right now how I knew that was God. Well, first of all, there are three sources from where you may get nudges, suggestions, or leadings. One is God, two is your own flesh (which is your own ideas) and third, the enemy of you; that would be Satan, the thief who comes to rob you of every good thing. So suggesting that I wash Spencer's feet wasn't coming from me (my flesh) because that was certainly something I had never thought of doing, nor was it something I *wanted* to do. I can't imagine Satan wanting me to wash my husband's feet, for that could be a good thing, and Satan only seeks to steal, kill, and destroy. I *knew* it was God, but I didn't accept the idea right away, that's for sure.

It's very important for me to be real. When I speak to women, whether it's in a large gathering or a Bible study group, my Sunday School class or one person sitting in my living room, I want them to know of my failures as much as my victories. I know that I admire and respect those most who are honest and real. That is why in relating my stories I tell you of my doubts, my struggles, my stupidity, and even my stubbornness or rebelliousness.

As the day went on, the Lord kept nudging my thoughts and my heart to wash Spencer's feet. He wouldn't let me alone about it. Even then, I was still questioning, *Is this really God asking me to do this?* Maybe I was just looking for an excuse to not have to do it.

Spencer came home from work. We had supper, and I washed the dishes and cleaned the kitchen. He'd settled into his recliner for an evening of television.

I cautiously approached the subject, beginning with, "Do you remember the scripture about Jesus washing the disciples' feet?"

"Yes, I remember. What about it?"

"Could we turn off the TV for a while? I want to talk to you."

He gave me one of those "Oh no, not one of those talks" kind of looks, but he agreed to turn off the TV. He then sat back down. "Okay," he said, "what do you want to talk about?"

"Well, I was asking you if you remembered the scripture about the foot washing."

"And I said, 'Yes, I remember.'" He looked at me, waiting for my reply.

"Okay, so would you let me wash your feet?"

Without hesitation, he said, "Why, do they stink?"

I thought nervously, *Okay, I'm off the hook. This must not be God wanting me to do this because my husband isn't going to let me, and he even made a joke about it.*

Just as I was finishing that thought, Spencer said, "Yes, I'll let you wash my feet."

What? Oh my gosh, it is God. Now what do I do? I had never washed *anyone's* feet before in a foot washing. I didn't know what to do. I guess I didn't think it was really going to happen. *I need a basin, water, towels, what else? Okay, Patty, get it together.*

My thoughts were churning out instructions.

I had no idea that I was walking into a divine appointment that evening in my living room. The hand of God was reaching down to heal hearts and a marriage.

I brought the basin of water over to Spencer as he was sitting forward in his recliner. I knelt by his feet. One of the things that struck me as I was gathering the needed items was that both he and I were quiet, almost reverent, as if something deeply spiritual was happening—and it was.

I removed his socks, picked up his foot, placed it in the warm water, then did the same with the other foot. I had no idea what I was supposed to say.

Then the words came, as I gently splashed the water onto his feet. "Lord, I'm thankful for every day this man has gone to work and never complained ..." It went on and on, words of love and appreciation flowing easily from me to him. My tears were dripping into the water as I washed his feet, with those tears. And Spencer's tears were dripping onto my head as I knelt beneath him. He kept repeating, "Blondie, please forgive me."

Fifteen years of hurt were washed away in a fifteen-minute foot washing; the scorecard destroyed.

God gave me an all-consuming love for my husband, one that sees Spencer as Christ sees him—his worth and value. He gave me that respect and love for Spencer that I had asked for. I was learning not to look at the deeds but see who he really was as a person. I truly was given a glimpse of how Christ sees each of us in our hearts.

As of this writing, we've celebrated forty-seven years of marriage, all by the grace of God. I no longer keep score of wrongs. When they happen, I try to always let them go right then, as I want my wrongs to be forgotten. Has it all been perfect? No, we are both imperfect beings, but that divine appointment with

God in attendance made us appreciate each other and our marriage. The glory belongs to a heavenly Father who wants His children to have the joy of the Lord in all areas of their lives.

One of the greatest lessons I learned: it was *me* that the Lord changed.

A snapshot of His grace.

> Delight yourself in the Lord, and He will give you the desires of your heart
>
> Psalm 37:4

> Many, O Lord my God, are the wonders which Thou hast done, and Thy thoughts towards us. There is none to compare with Thee; if I would declare and speak of them, they would be too numerous to count.
>
> Psalm 40:5

The Rescue

> And God is able to make all grace abound to you, so that in all things, at all times, having all that you need, you will abound in every good work.
>
> 2 Corinthians 9:8 (NIV)

I knew I had a long drive ahead of me. The drive to Albany, Georgia, from my home in Oklahoma to speak at a women's retreat was over a thousand miles.

My first day on the road, I chose to travel on I-40 east to make better time. However, running into road construction on the interstate slowed me down a lot. I got off of the interstate and went to a motel for the night. The next morning I decided to look for an alternate route, finding out that the construction was in several states I needed to drive through.

After breakfast, I began driving down small roads exploring, if you will, alternatives to the interstate but each time only to find construction. The last road I chose to explore took me a little farther away from the town I had stayed in the night before. I continued on, thinking I would surely come to a major highway that would parallel the interstate. This, of course, was before GPS.

As I drove on, traffic got lighter until there was no one but me on the road. Topping a hill, I saw way off in the distance more construction and idle equipment sitting there. I stopped, looking for a place to turn around. There was a half-moon dirt and gravel area on my left, so I backed in—bad decision. I had spent the night in Mississippi, which had had a lot of rain, getting a picture, yet? As I was backing into the half-moon area, I heard and felt a *kerplunk.* All of a sudden, the nose of my minivan was up in the air, and the back of my van had somewhat disappeared.

I climbed out to assess the situation. My van had been swallowed up in a sinkhole, buried up to the back window—not good. I got back into the van, looked around, and saw no one. I picked up my cell phone—no service. I put my head on the steering wheel and prayed a sentence prayer (that's a prayer that doesn't go into a lot of detail, keeping it just to a sentence). My sentence was, "Lord, help me," short and sweet. I was thinking, *Now what are you going to do, stupid?*

I heard an approaching noise and looked up. There was a truck coming down the road I'd turned off of to turn around. The truck had a wench on the front of it—a *wench,* I said. A male driver glanced to his left and did a double-take then stopped suddenly, backed up, and turned in toward me. I climbed out. He got out and started walking toward me. "Found yourself a nice little hole, didn't you, little lady?"

Laughing, I said, "Yes, I sure did."

He walked to the back of the van. "Whoa, you're swallowed clean up to your window."

I put my hand out to shake his hand, saying, "Thank you so much for stopping. I'm Patty. Please tell me your name is Angel."

He kind of chuckled. "No, ma'am, it's Carl."

"Well, I still think it's Angel. I had just prayed. It hadn't been more than a couple of minutes, and you drove up. I'm a Christian, so I was praying for God to help me."

"I figured you were a Christian when I saw your *JESUS* license plate on the front of your van, which was sticking up in the air, hard to miss. I'll hook on to your van, and I'll have you out in a jiffy. Then we'll see what kind of damage you have."

While he was hooking his wench to my van, he asked where I was headed. I told him I'd driven from Oklahoma and was speaking and singing at a women's retreat in Georgia.

He told me to get in the van and to just keep the tires straight for him to pull it forward. Within a couple of minutes, I was free from the hole. Yeah!

We walked to the back of my van. It was covered with good ole red clay, but there was no damage whatsoever. Wow!

Walking back to the front, he looked at me and said, "You know, you calling me Angel was pretty special. Even though it's not my name, I know God had something to do with this."

I said to him, "I'm sure of it."

He went on, "I was with my crew at Denny's this morning having breakfast. We kinda discuss the day's work. My boss told me he didn't want me to go with the rest of the crew, but wanted to send me somewhere else. He said there was a piece of equipment, a dirt mover, that a guy wanted to sell and asked me to go take a look at it. He drew directions to this road, the road right here." He pointed to the road in front of us. "You see that machine down the road there sitting off to the side? Well, that's where I was going. But now I know that's not why I was out here. God sent me here to rescue you." He pointed at me. He got a little teary as he said, "I'm a Christian too, but I've kind of neglected God lately. To think that He picked me, who had a truck with a wench on it, and sent me out here to find you to pull you out of that hole. Then to find out that you are a sister in Christ, wow, that just blows me away. Just when I start wondering whether God even knows where I am, He goes and proves, that He does."

I gave him a hug as he told me it meant so much to him to know that God still wanted to use him and needed him. He then handed me his card with his number on it, saying, "On your way back from Georgia, if you have a problem, you give me a call." We both laughed.

Two people who had never met, God brought together—one with a need (me) and one a "need-meeter" (that would be Angel, I mean Carl). God is the orchestrator. To Him belongs all the glory. His love went all the way to where I was, in a very deep hole, a long way from home.

Keep reading another snapshot of grace—the rest of the story.

> For He will command His angels concerning you
> to guard you in all your ways;
>
> Psalm 91:11 (NIV)

The Return Trip

> I pray that you will begin to understand how incredibly great His power is to help those who believe Him.
>
> Ephesians 1:19 (TLB)

It was a beautiful day as I left on my return trip to my home in Oklahoma after speaking at a weekend retreat. I decided to choose a different route, one that would take me through Alabama using state highways, remembering the construction on the interstate and the delays it had caused on my trip down to Georgia.

As it turned out, that decision put me in a violent thunderstorm just as I arrived in Birmingham, Alabama. The rain was coming down in torrents. My windshield wipers couldn't keep up with the downpour, dangerously restricting my view, and the wind was rocking my minivan. Traffic was very congested, and it was almost impossible to see anything, much less the other cars on the road.

My thought as I was trying to watch traffic was, *Why in the world did I come this way?*

My anxiety level was escalating just as I spotted a Burger King on the right. I pulled in to get out of the madness of the traffic. I sat in the van taking deep breaths, trying to calm down after a couple of near misses with other drivers.

It wasn't even noon yet, but I thought I could go in and get a drink and wait to see if the storm would let up. Before getting out of my van, I grabbed an umbrella, saying a quick prayer, "Lord, I know that You know right where I am. I made a mistake when I chose this route, but I need Your peace that I'm going to be okay despite the storm. Thank You for hearing me, and I love You."

Walking in, I saw a rather long line of people waiting to order, so I joined them. I felt a soft tap on my shoulder and, turning around, saw a couple standing in line behind me. The man said, "Hi. We were just wondering, didn't you get out of that white minivan?"

"Yes, I sure did."

He asked, "Aren't you from Ponca City, Oklahoma?"

Bewildered, I replied, "Yes, I am. How did you know that? Is it written on me somewhere?" I pulled out my T-shirt to see if the writing on it said "Ponca City" anywhere. It didn't.

They laughed, saying, "No, we saw your license plate was from Kay County in Oklahoma. We used to live there."

Astonished, I said, "Are you kidding me? You lived in Ponca?"

They nodded yes, and then he said, "I was the pastor at St. Luke's Nazarene Church there." He introduced himself and his wife.

"Oh my gosh, I have a lot of friends who go to that church."

They knew several of the same people I did. After telling them my name, I asked them if they now lived in Birmingham. He told me that he'd been pastoring a church for several years in Birmingham, but they had loved their years in Ponca City. Then he said to me, "So what are you doing in Birmingham today?" I told him that I had been speaking at a women's retreat in Georgia and was on my way back to Oklahoma. "Boy, you're driving in quite a storm, and you may be in it for a while."

"That's why I pulled in here. It was getting too hard for me to see to drive."

His wife spoke up, "Us too. We had gone to do some errands, and it got really bad really fast."

Looking at me, he said, "Would it be okay with you if my wife and I had a prayer with you?"

"You bet."

The three of us joined hands, standing in line at a Burger King in Birmingham, Alabama. He prayed a beautiful prayer for me, for safety in my travel, for God's hand on me, and for His angels to be around my van to keep me safe. The he prayed, "And Lord, most of all give Patty Your peace that she will be okay in spite of the storm." The *very* words I had prayed just before coming into the restaurant.

Count your blessings; name them one by one.

Think on this. I changed my route—God knew.

I ran into a storm in Birmingham, Alabama.

I prayed for His peace, and He answered by sending a pastor to the same restaurant I had randomly picked, who coincidentally had lived in my hometown of Ponca City, Oklahoma, and who now lived in Birmingham and also picked the same restaurant at the same moment to pull into, who then prayed for me using the exact words I had used in my prayer for God's peace.

Coincidence? I don't think so. In fact, I know it wasn't. God, in His divine mercy, met my need. I have done nothing to deserve His constant care for me. It's not about who I am; it's about *whose* I am. I belong to Him. I have given my life to Him. That is available to *all.*

A footnote for you: another blessing of this encounter didn't dawn on me until months later. We don't actually reside in Kay County. Our home is just outside of Kay County, about eight miles, in Osage County, but still part of Ponca City. We had tagged all of our vehicles in Osage County, *except* for one.

Yep, you guessed it ... my white minivan. We had purchased it used from an individual who did live in Kay County, so that's the county the van was tagged in. That pastor and his wife might not have recognized an Osage County tag but certainly the Kay County one where they'd made their home. A snapshot of grace to be sure.

The following are quotes from "The Father's Love Letter" (Anonymous).

It is My desire to lavish My love on you.

1 John 3:1

Simply because you are My child and I am your Father.

I John 3:1

Every good gift that you receive comes from My hand.

James 1:17

For I am your provider and I meet all your needs.

Matthew 6:31–33

Because I love you with an everlasting love.

Jeremiah 3:13

I will never stop doing good to you.

Jeremiah 32:40

For you are My treasured possession.

Exodus 19:5

If you seek Me with all your heart you will find Me.

Deuteronomy 4:29

Never Underestimate the Value of a Hug

He has given me a new song to sing, of praises to our God. Now many will hear of the glorious things He did for me, and stand in awe before the Lord, and put their trust in Him.

Psalm 40:3 (TLB)

One of the greatest lessons I have learned about the value of each of us was through a lady in a nursing home.

In the early days of my singing ministry, I went to nursing homes. I started out just going into individual rooms, plopping down in a chair, and singing to the resident. I was never turned away; however, I realized I had a *captive* audience.

During this same period of time, the Lord had given me an idea for starting a crisis phone line for teens. I was already a volunteer for an information line called Helpline, also serving on the Board of Directors. I presented the idea to the board about an additional phone line for teens. With their approval, we moved forward. I named the project Teenline. Teenline was very successful but demanded a lot more of my time, as I served as the coordinator for two and a half years. This affected my time to sing at the four nursing homes in Ponca City.

Not wanting to give up the entire nursing home ministry, I decided to choose just one home, once a week. Every Thursday morning you'd find me at Shawn Manor Nursing Home. This continued for over ten years.

Instead of going to the individual rooms, we decided to have the residents come to the chapel for the program. Some friends joined me to be part of reaching out to the residents. There would be anywhere from twenty-five to fifty residents in attendance each week. We invited pastors to come and speak as well as musicians and soloists to be a part of the ministry to the residents there.

As people would call to volunteer to sing or play an instrument, I would welcome them and thank them for their willingness to share their talent, but I would also ask, "After you share your talent, please don't leave. We want you to stay until the end of the program. At the end we go out and hug on all the residents because they need to know they are loved, they're not forgotten, and they are valuable."

One Thursday morning as we closed the program, preparing to go out and give hugs, I noticed a new resident. She wasn't sitting with the others. She had pulled her wheelchair up to the wall and was peeking around the wall, listening to the music. I thought, *Oh, there's a new person. I'll go give her a hug,* thinking everybody liked being hugged. Well, I found out that doesn't necessarily apply.

I approached her, leaning down to hug her. She reached up and very hatefully and briskly shoved me away, saying, "You leave me alone. I don't want you to hug me!" I'll admit to you, it hurt my feelings, but I had two choices of what I could do with those hurt feelings. I could say, "Okay, lady, see if I ever try to hug you again." Or I could take those hurt feelings to the *One* who could make a difference. I chose the latter.

Driving home, I prayed, "Lord, you know what's made this woman bitter, what has shut her heart. Could you please give me the key to her heart to unlock the joy I know can be there?" Every Thursday morning, I would sit in the parking lot of Shawn Manor Nursing Home and pray before I went in. I would also sing, "Make me a blessing, make me a blessing, out of my life, let Jesus shine." I'd go in with expectancy that maybe today would be the day.

We'd begin the program. I would see her pull up and peek around the wall, and I'd think, *Maybe today's the day.* Hug time would come, and I'd walk toward her, she'd see me coming and hold up her hand, saying, "You leave me alone. I don't want nothing to do with you."

"Okay, so today's not the day," I would whisper to myself.

This went on for several weeks. I asked those who ran the nursing home if they could tell me something about her.

They asked, "What would you like to know?"

"Well, do you know if she's a Christian?"

"She says she is, but actually she's just a mean old biddy."

All righty then, I'll have to get out my mean old biddy prayers.

One Thursday morning, it was my turn to sing. I was in the middle of the song, and I saw her pull up to the edge of the wall. *There she is... today's the day, go for her.* It was like a ticker tape message running across my thoughts. I knew it was the Lord communicating with me, giving me His thoughts. I turned off my music in the middle of the song, and I headed for her.

She saw me coming. I must have looked more determined than ever because she didn't hold up her hand to stop me. She grabbed the wheels of her chair and began rolling backwards to get away from me. At this point, I was not running, but I *was* pursuing with a mission.

All the other residents were wondering what was going on, whispering, "Why did she quit singing? Where's she going?" It was like an E.F. Hutton moment. Hearing their whispers as I walked by, I thought to myself, *You know, it doesn't matter what anybody thinks. God has a divine appointment with a lady's heart.* She was still rolling backwards, rolling, rolling, rolling, getting farther away from me. Then she said loudly, in the same hateful voice, "You're not gonna try to hug me again, are you?"

I just stopped and said, "No, ma'am, I'm not." Right at that moment, God dropped the answer into my heart, which was the key to her heart that I had asked for.

Looking at her, I said, "You know what? I haven't had a very good morning, and I sure could use a hug from *you.*"

Those wheels stopped dead in their tracks, and with a voice that was softened, she looked at me and said, "What did you say?" I knew God was at work in her heart as I heard that softness in her voice.

I repeated, "I haven't had a good morning, and I really do need a hug—from you."

She opened her arms and said, "Honey, come here." She let me in.

I went to her, bent down to hug her, and she enveloped me. I let her hold on to me as long as she wanted to. I knew it had been a long time since she'd let anyone get that close to her. My chin was on her shoulder, and her chin rested on mine. She whispered in my ear, "Oh, this feels so good."

As I stood up, I said, "Yes, ma'am, it sure does, and I have a question for you."

With a smile that went from ear to ear and sweet tears passing over the smile, she said, "What's the question?"

I asked her, as I'm asking you, the reader, "Do you have any idea how much God loves you and how valuable *you* are?"

I say to you who are reading this, "Get your heart and your mind wrapped around that, if you can."

Widening her smile, she answered, "I didn't know that, but I do now. When you told me that you needed for me to hug you, you told me I had something to give, that I had value." That one tiny sentence was just what she needed to hear, and only God knew what she needed in her heart. God knows each of us because He created us and knows each of us intimately.

That lady became the resident hugger of Shawn Manor Nursing Home. God unfolded her like a flower, and she was a joy to be around. Those of us who were part of the ministry there became aware of how seriously she took her hugging ministry. She posted herself by the front door and required a hug from all who entered.

One Thursday morning, while we were having our program, she was sitting in her wheelchair by the door. A maintenance man came in, and all he wanted to do was change a lightbulb. He had his overalls on and was carrying a ladder, ready to get to work, but she wouldn't let him pass until he hugged her. He finally relented, hugged her, and she let him pass.

It was so funny to watch. He got hugged whether he wanted it or not, but I'm sure it made his day go better.

What made her so bitter? Family never came to visit her. She felt hurt, invisible, and totally devalued as a person. God didn't change the circumstances; He changed her in the circumstances.

Value is set by the price someone is willing to pay for something. We are so highly valued by God that He gave the very best He had to pay that high price. He gave His only Son for you and for me. No one in this world will ever love you or value you like your heavenly Father. You may get your value from your job, whom you're married to, what kind of house you live in, what kind of car you drive, how much money you have, etcetera. But all of those things *will change.* God says, "For I the Lord do not change" (Malachi 3:6). Your value doesn't lie in the things or people in your life. Your value was established when God created you.

> O Lord, You have examined my heart and You know everything about me. You know when I sit or stand. When far away You know my every thought. You chart the path ahead of me and tell me where to stop and rest. Every moment, You know where I am. You know what I am going to say before I even say it. You both precede and follow me, and place Your hand of blessing on my head. This is too glorious, too wonderful to believe. I can never be lost to Your spirit! I can never get away from my God. If I go up to heaven, You are there, if I go down to the place of the dead, You are there. If I ride the morning winds to the farthest oceans, even there Your hand will guide me, Your strength will support me. If I try to hide in darkness, the night becomes light around me. For even darkness cannot hide from God; to You the night shines as bright as day. Darkness and light are both alike to You. You made all the delicate, inner parts of my body, and knit them together in my mother's womb. Thank You for making me so wonderfully complex. It is amazing to think about. Your workmanship is marvelous and how well I know it. You were there while I was being formed

> in utter seclusion. You saw me before I was born and scheduled each day of my life before I began to breathe. Every day was recorded in Your book. How precious it is, Lord to realize that You are thinking about me constantly! I can't even count how many times a day Your thoughts turn towards me. And when I wake in the morning You are still thinking of me.
>
> Psalm 139:1–18 (TLB)

> Search me, O God, and know my heart; test my thoughts. Point out anything You find in me that makes You sad, and lead me along the path of everlasting life.
>
> Psalm 139:23 (TLB)

This is what your heavenly Father thinks of you: you *are* one of a kind. Before you were born, there was never anyone like you, and after you're gone, there will never be another you. You are uniquely and wonderfully made, and God does have a plan and a purpose for your life. You are His snapshot of grace. And He has many divine appointments for you to experience.

Afterword

The book you have just finished reading is just paper and black print, unless, you have sensed the hand of God on you as you've read of His undeserved grace on an ordinary life.

As you read my account of finding the true love relationship we were intended to have, before we were even born, hopefully you discovered that the emptiness you may have felt is that disconnect from your Creator, like an itch you couldn't scratch, something missing and you didn't know what. You've tried to fill that empty void with everything the world has to offer, but nothing you have tried lasts. I was there, I know what truly fills that void in all of us, and it is the love of God. It may sound hokey, but it is true—I am living proof, and I am head-over-heels in love with my Lord and not ashamed to say it. No, I'm not a fanatic. I'm just a person who found the answer we all look for, and it literally has given me life. God loves us; tall or short, fat or thin, smart or not, He chooses us. You don't have to stand in line, waiting to be chosen.

The Lord waits for you. He is waiting for His turn, for your attention. Is it time?

These are the treasures that await you.

Freedom to not wear masks anymore, no pretending—you can be you. God knows our faults, and He loves us and helps us strive to become the people we need to be.

You will no longer have to look for approval but have a sense of belonging and know that we do belong to something greater than anything we see.

A love that stays the same, does not fluctuate either forward or backward, up or down—it's unchanging—as His child. He doesn't move; only we move away from Him.

Peace with God, peace with ourselves, and peace with others.

You will have someone to go to when no one else understands—He does—and know why we're here and where we'll spend eternity.

I pray right now for you, as you read these words, that you'll want that relationship with God through believing and accepting Jesus Christ, His Son, into your heart and life. Remember this: no other deity has pursued man to have a personal relationship with Him but God, through Christ. You mean that much to Him.

Should you want to give your life back to God and you believe that Christ is who He says He is, I have provided this prayer for you to pray, if you truly believe in your heart and you want to put your past behind you and become a brand-new creation.

"Lord, I've recognized my need for You. I know I have sinned and not been what I should be. Please forgive me of those sins. I've been selfish to want to live my life my way, rather than living the life You had planned for me. I believe that You sent your Son, Jesus, to die on a cross for me because You love me, and I believe He went to the grave for me and rose three days later to show man that we too can conquer death as Jesus did. Now, I ask Christ to become my Savior and to live in my heart, to live His life through me. I thank you, Lord, that today I have eternal life."

Welcome to the family of God, you are loved!

If you don't own a Bible, purchase one that's easy for you to read. That was key for me as a new Christian. I needed wording that I could relate to and understand, at least to start me off right. After you buy it, begin in the Book of John in the New Testament and become acquainted with Jesus. Psalms and Proverbs in the Old Testament fill you with hope and wisdom about life situations. Walk with God, my friend, and become all you can be for Him.

See you in heaven one day.

I'm just one of God's signposts pointing the way with love.

For the readers who already have this precious relationship, *rejoice,* along with me, over those who have joined us as brothers and sisters in Christ and for those who have stored all of this in their hearts. Pray that the seeds of these snapshots of grace and the meaning behind the stories—that God cares for His own—will grow in their spirit so they will seek to know Christ in an ever deeper way, and I thank you for your prayers for them. I pray that God would keep them and *you* in His care. May God bless you and make His face to shine upon you.

> For God loved the world so much that He gave His only Son so that anyone who believes in Him shall not perish but have eternal life.
>
> John 3:16 (TLB)